COPYRIGHT © 2025 Nell P.

Printed in the United States of America

First Printing Edition, 2025

ISBN 979-8-90046-971-3

Table of Contents

Preface   3

Forward   4

Chapter One: How It All Started   6

Chapter Two: Nowhere Else to Go   24

Chapter Three: At-A-Glance   41

Chapter Four: It's About Her   56

Chapter Five: It's About Him (The Protector and Hustler)   77

Chapter Six: It's About Him (The Abuser)   96

Chapter Seven: It's About Him (The Man and His Addiction)   112

Chapter Eight: Mental Note   127

Chapter Nine: I'm Confused   141

Chapter Ten: It's Not About Me   153

Chapter Eleven: What About the Baby?   164

Chapter Twelve: A Light Drizzle   179

Chapter Thirteen: A Light Drizzle, Part II   190

Chapter Fourteen: The Unseen   212

Chapter Fifteen: The Unseen, Part II   236

Chapter Sixteen: The Unseen, Part III (I Forgot to Mention)   264

Chapter Seventeen: The In-Between   286

Chapter Eighteen: The Sunken Place   330

Chapter Nineteen: The Sunken Place, Part II   355

Chapter Twenty: The Sunken Place, Part III: Refusal   385

Chapter Twenty-One: The Sunken Place, Part IV: Mourning   412

Chapter Twenty-Two: Released   439

Preface

In writing this memoir I wanted to capture the essence of my life's journey. Reflecting on the significant moments that have shaped me into the person I am today. The memories contained within these pages are a tapestry of joy, sorrow, triumph, and strength. It is my hope that through sharing my stories, readers will find moments of connection, inspiration, and understanding in their own lives. My memoir is a testament to the power of resilience and the beauty of my release party.

When I say 'release party,' I'm not talking about balloons or confetti. It's my personal term for what writing poetry has been to me. Poetry became the place where I could release the weight I carried, the thoughts and emotions I had to keep bottled up in everyday life. Through writing, I gave myself permission to feel, to process, and to heal. 'Release Party' is how I maintained my sanity and found freedom in expression when silence felt safer than speaking. It's not just my story, it's a tribute to the shared experiences that bind us all together.

#ReleaseParty

Foreword

There is a rare breed of writers who possess a dynamic and captivating style that sets them apart from the rest. They have a raw talent that ignites the pages, drawing readers into a world where imagination knows no bounds. Nell P. is such a writer, one whose words possess an unparalleled power to resonate deeply within the hearts of readers.

Through her exceptional storytelling and compelling narratives, Nell P. offers a fresh and invigorating perspective on life. Her writing is infused with a distinct and thought-provoking outlook that challenges conventional notions, forcing readers to question the status quo. In this hybrid poetry memoir, Nell P. blurs the boundaries by blending memory and metaphor, truth and art. She has created a space where lived experience and poetic expression coexist unapologetically. With every turn of the page, readers are transported into a realm where the extraordinary intertwines seamlessly with the mundane, binding emotions into art and experiences that leave an indelible mark.

My connection with Nell P. spans over two decades, a journey of friendship and collaboration that has allowed me to witness her growth and evolution. From stumbling upon her talent in the early days all the way through to the present, it has been a privilege to bear witness to the strength and perseverance that permeate her work. Through personal victories and triumphs, as well as moments of vulnerability and introspection, Nell P. has emerged as a force to be reckoned with in the literary world. In this collection of Nell P.'s work, you will find yourself transported to worlds filled with magic, vulnerability, and unyielding hope. Prepare to be challenged, comforted, and, above all, moved by the extraordinary storytelling prowess of this remarkable writer.

Janell

Release Party

The Only Way Out

CHAPTER ONE

How It All Started

When I look back on my life, I now see

that things weren't always as they appeared to be

We had nice things... house, car, clothes, and more

We even had a little backyard shed candy store

All was well when I was a child

Roasting marshmallows in the backyard

Playing kickball in the street with friends

Having our dinner then going to bed

All was right in the world, or so it seemed

Then the bright sky was covered by a storm cloud

What happened to the light?

Why is the dark so frightening?

What once was will no longer be...

I was young; none of this made sense to me

It would just be a brief vacation, he said

A family road trip is what he said

The summer was starting, time to get away

We were heading up North to visit family for a few days

That short-lived truth quickly changed

When we stayed past three days

What was going on? None of us really knew

What I knew was that this wasn't home

This place I didn't want to be

A foreign land to my siblings and I

How were we to survive in this unfamiliar place?

Why did he bring us here?

Why do we have to stay?

"On the Road Again" became my favorite song

Have you ever been in a situation that was difficult

to understand?

Imagine going to bed without a decent meal

Can you imagine how cramped it is to sleep in a car?

Well, imagine a family of six in that car

Packed with what has now

Become your life

Bringing enough for a weekend trip only to find

That these items would be your everyday

No plan in place upon our arrival

Just us trying to figure it out, like an episode of Survival

So much time had passed and the season had changed

Northern weather, to me, is nothing shy of strange

How would you feel being four feet tall

Walking in three feet of snow?

My tears where afraid to roll down my face

This muff, that I called my furry igloo, was my only

warm place

My hands were indeed warm as supposed to the

remaining

Parts of me that seemed frozen in time as I walked these streets

The car, which was home, is now gone

Towed away from a no parking zone

Therefore, we walked endlessly

Knowing that you couldn't stop because that was the only way to get

to where you needed to go

Although we muscled up the strength to walk from place to place

Where ever we ended up, there was no guarantee we were going to stay any longer than a few days

The warmth felt inside any of those buildings was short-lived but it helped anyway

We bounced from family to hotel to the back storage room of a store

The space was either crowded or dingy and gloomy

We were no longer in our rural neighborhood back home

Where we could go from our Mamie to our Mimi's

house

By just dashing through the woods

There were buildings beside buildings

And traffic was everywhere

Allowing a few southern country kids to roam these

streets

Would have been a grave injustice

Unfamiliarity to this new environment led us to

confinement

No socializing, no friends, no more playing kickball

in the street

We were happy if we got a decent plate of food to eat

I can remember asking myself "When will it all be

over?"

Day after day I questioned where we were going to stay

Sneaking into motel rooms

Sleeping in different cars that my parents obtained over time

Wanting to go to family, but it was way too far

Looking at different places pondering what would be

Is it vacant? Is it occupied?

This place looks abandoned to me

This old abandoned house is where we would sleep

Occupied by many, but there was still one vacant bedroom

It was a three-level home and our bedroom was on the second floor

One bed, one sitting chair, one window, and nothing more

The children's bed was a single blanket on a wooden floor

It wasn't nice or neat nor was it pretty

But it was better than the motel down

the hill in the middle of crack city

This was our resting place, for now

We had nowhere else to go

Home wasn't an option…

Why? I didn't know

We lived in this filth awfully long

My mother got tired and couldn't take it anymore

She cleaned only God knows what out the one and

only bathroom

Dead rodents and feces And a whole lot more

So her kids could wash without standing on that

nasty floor

Abandoned? Yes, but occupied by many

This place was now called home

Home… really?

Being a mother is hard enough without the added trouble

Every child is equivalent to one job in itself

Cooking, feeding, cleaning, chastising, and nurturing with every breath

It's hard to do, seemingly so little and more than enough

Standing by her man through thick and thin

Knowing that she had to be there, unsure when it would end

Making sure the kids were OK and helping them understand...

Dad has a problem, but he is a good man

Teaching me from books she found on the street

Many nights going without so her kids could eat

A mother's love that is what she instilled in me!

I'm a mother because she was a mother...

I don't know how else to be

He was the man. He was everything to me

He was my protector, and he wouldn't let anything happen to me

He was Superman, Man of Steel

His words, his attitude, his character couldn't be beat

He was untouchable

In my eyes, that's all I could see

He did wrong, but it wasn't really that wrong to me

We all knew he didn't have much money

But he knew that his family had to eat

So I never questioned when he brought back canned goods and meat

He sometimes explained his actions to me

"It was wrong of me to put my hands on things that didn't belong to me"

"But I am a man that has to feed his family"

Those words I understood

If he didn't feed his family, who else would?

This is my daddy, people!

Can't you see he loves me unconditionally?

He was my voice of wisdom

He could handle anything

He was Superman... Man of Steel

But even Superman had his kryptonite and so did my dad

He shot it up every night, faithfully

We went through a great deal of adversity, we were so close

Close enough to withstand the stormy weather

Although the situation was bad

One part was good – we were family

And that closeness was as it should be

If one hurt, we all hurt

If one cried, we all cried

This is how we were raised to be

If one fights, we all fight

No one is ever to hurt our family

This is how it was, but changed over time

As everyone got older and aspired to get away

They became guarded and selfish

The envied how people they knew lived

They seemed to care more about what they could get instead of give

I could understand why they wanted to get away

I just couldn't understand why our love couldn't remain

That close-knit family was left behind

I was no longer theirs

And they were no longer mine

What really happened?

I don't think I will ever understand

Never really know why

That bond slipped away

Why would we never be as close as we were in those early days?

When I cried, they no longer cried with me

But when they hurt I still hurt

That's how I was raised to be

Everyone deals with life in vastly different ways

The tragedy... the hurt... it creates different shades

I was young and I was unable to see

Just what shade I was going to be

I believe it spanned just over a year

Though it seemed like forever

The days felt like months

And the months felt like years

Everything intertwined during our time here

We shared so many tears throughout that time

But as I sat in the airport waiting for our flight to go back

home

My mind recapped the events that occurred over time

We walked so many streets

We went to bed most nights with little or nothing to eat

We snuck in and out of hotel rooms, trying to dodge a

large bill

We stayed in the back of a store... Anything to get off

the streets

All this time had passed

And it finally seemed like it was coming to an end

The storm was over

We were finally going to be set free

Free from the pain, the hurt, the poverty

Weren't we...?

And so we left, to regain what we had

House, car, nice things like we had in the beginning

I wondered if we would re-open our backyard candy store

The life I knew before was coming around again

As Willie Nelson's record spun in my head

Finally, we were on our way home

The nightmare had come to an end

I was so happy that the bad stuff was over

When we got back, I thought, things would be better

But it turned out this year away was a ridiculously small piece of how it all started

A blink of an eye

A snap of the fingers

Although there were many more storms I endured

I just decided to take a few drops from the winners

The events that transformed me

Small pieces from the stories of my life that caused me to question why

Events that made we wonder if this life was worth living

The impending storm was way bigger and so much longer

It had a lasting impact

My life was forever changed

And I had to figure out how to deal with that pain

Life is life...

It's not all good nor all bad

You deal with the situations whether happy or sad

You can't predict what will come or what will go

But there's one thing I know...

It will surely help you grow!

How you choose to grow is solely on you ... Good or bad Life is Life

... It can't tell you what to do

Of course, I stumbled along my journey

But Life is Life and I choose to live it My Way

So welcome to my world

This is how I coped

I was unable to speak

So therefore, I wrote

CHAPTER TWO

NOWHERE ELSE TO GO

There was so much anticipation as we were in the air

Maybe the flight was beautiful, but I didn't really care

All that mattered to me was that I was on my way back home

On touchdown there was a noticeable change

The temperature, the scenery, the smiling faces

We arrived back to our home state and went straight to my dad's mom's house

She was the pillar of the family, we called her Mamie

There we were greeted by many

It was so warm and inviting

A meal was prepared and ready for us to eat

For the past year or more I'd only seen this in my sleep

I missed Mamie's face as well as her cooking

I missed playing with my cousins and our neighborhood friends

To see all those we missed we made our way around

And were welcomed by all, who had missed us in turn

Life would be different now

Things would be better

We would get back what we had

No more stormy weather

I thought it was gone, but it was just taking a break

Things looked different but were ultimately unchanged

As time went by our family members didn't act the same

The smiles went away

People began to change; they started to complain

No, the living situation wasn't as bad as it had been

But still looked in some ways the same

We all were in a single room here

At least in our abandoned home we had privacy

But not in these family members' homes, that was plain to see and hear

We had daily reminders that we had nothing in these places

After all that hoping and wishing...

What did we really come back to?

Here again came the hurt and the pain, but worse

Now came the truth...

And the truth was a devastating thang!

Once again we went from house to house

Looking for ways out of terribly similar situations

The generosity of others was short-lived

We would quickly become a burden...

These grown folks with four kids

Things can surely change over time

The wider family I thought I had wasn't very kind

They talked about us and some just flat out lied

One had the audacity to say that I told them that I didn't love my dad

Another commented that my big brother must be gay

Simply because of how he spoke

Obviously proper grammar is strictly for those kinds of folks

This instability caused all kinds of grief

How are we to respect individuals who speak such things about children?

But even in the midst of the distress I was grateful

We at least had a decent place to sleep

The process was slow

My Superman was tired and frustrated

But determined to find us Our Own Home

My mom found a job

My dad did what he did to make ends meet

We were no longer living with others

Nor were we living on the street

We were in a two-bedroom house now

It wasn't huge but enough

The type of work Dad did wasn't... well, conventional

But it provided him with money

To feed his habit first and then his kids

Mom found help from churches, food banks, and non-profits

That help with food, clothes, furniture, and even bills

Things should have been alright... Right?

But they weren't, for reasons unknown

For sights I don't ever recall seeing...

It came like a thief in the night

And it didn't plan on leaving

There was an argument and then a fight

It sounded like lightning when he struck her

She cried and we cried as he went out the door

Why did it happen?

Why was he in such an uproar?

She didn't do anything...

So why is her face now sore?

I didn't understand why he would do such a thing

How was she supposed to go to work?

How can she have a black and blue eye?

How is she supposed to act like it doesn't hurt?

Maybe he just lost control?

Superman was supposed to protect us, not hurt us

(I felt for her!

I also felt for him!)

It came like a thief in the night and it did not leave

This night was put on repeat

Because this wasn't the only night my mom got beat

Then things went from bad to worse

Our living situation would constantly change

Our so-called family (some of them, anyway)

Shunned us and called us names

Told lies about us, used our name in vain

I didn't know what we did to these people

But they disliked us all the same

It wasn't as clear to us then as it is now

But we knew when we were treated differently

We always stood out

We were picked on because of how we talked

(We still spoke with a bit of northern slang)

We were considered weird because we showed respect

To and for our elders

We couldn't speak to them as if they were our peers

Yes, I will admit, everything about us was set us apart

Regardless of our circumstances, our lack of bare necessities

We walked with our heads held high

We gave the utmost respect to the ones who gave us life

And because of that fact we "didn't fit"

I didn't know that everyone in this world had to be the same

I didn't know all people had to blend in

Because we were raised with expectations

We were expected to act decent

We were a part of a constant competition...

So, when I say it went from bad to worse, please believe me

Your hell and my hell may be different

But it's hell just the same

Our time with others was limited

And even then, there were only certain ones we could be around

It was as if we weren't supposed to have fun

We were always serious any time my dad was home

Few, if any, were allowed to our home

Sometimes not even in the yard

Sometimes I think growing up was way too hard

I've never been sure why he was so strict

With nowhere to go all we could do was just sit...

And wonder what these walls would say if they could speak

Would they cry out for help for us or merely weep?

If these walls could speak God only knows what they would say

Would they account for every tear that was shed?

Would they tell who cried out and wished they were dead?

Did they keep count of all the bumps

And bruises my mother received?

Would they tell how many times we were woken from our sleep?

Or how many days we went to bed with nothing to eat?

Was this a home or a prison?

We were just surviving... not living

As we grew older, my siblings moved further away from me

That bond we shared was no longer, it seemed

But I did see that they began to hide things

They were influenced by outsiders... Obviously

We weren't raised to keep secrets, we were family

It seemed family was no longer important

It was all about their friends

People who didn't know or care how their days would begin or end

How can a person be your friend when they don't know your truth

I started to understand what my daddy said

"People and their habits will rub off on you in the end"

If you spend enough time with them, it will happen

I saw that more and more with every lie they told

Although they would always get caught, it never seemed to get old

I would cry every time the oldest two got in trouble

I still hurt when they hurt

I still cried when they cried

But I never understood why my siblings would lie

Words were no longer exchanged

I was the youngest of the lineup and I believed their every word

Now their lies were told to me

Making me think that my dad was wrong, but

Knowing that he knew exactly what was happening

It was always the second born that actually got caught

But because she was the younger of the two

He figured she was mimicking what she saw the oldest one do

There seemed to be no remorse for the things that they had done

The apologies were empty

They were said so he would no longer speak

Through all of the prior turmoil, I always felt like we were ok

Because we had each other

We were our own little support system

We held each other up...

At least before things began to change

They're only about "self" and not "us" these days

At every corner there were locked doors

No feelings were expressed

No opinions were given

Communal time no longer existed

They began to go their own separate ways

Now there's nothing or no one worth missing

No siblings to bond with and no such thing as friends

With nowhere to go, who knows how this will end

The first born is now of age and gone on to marry

The second born, like her friend, decided she was going

To run away from home

The third in line, my brother, was always in his own little world

Reality never really set in with him...

Meaning there was little to get from him

I was never sure why they decided to cope in this way

We all went through the same things

There was no reason for them to act out like this

Why did she run away? What was she running to?

They made me believe it was all our dad

Yes, he had his ways

I guess they didn't want to do what he said

Although his methods of raising us were unconventional

I believe the route he took was to make sure his kids could

Withstand the ways of this world

To make sure that if they fell down they could and would

Get back up after every fall

His method meant we could stand on our own two feet

And by this world we wouldn't be beat

So his demands were reasonable

His expectations were not that hard to understand

Being a respectable young woman just wasn't in their plans

As the family unit became smaller

Living in the home became even harder

Although it's sad to say, I had an older brother, but

He wasn't "that" big brother

He stayed in his world and I in mine

Dad began to lash out at me and I was at a loss to why

This was the same guy I rode with day and night

Many times, my rest was in the backseat of a car

The days came and went just like before

And with nowhere to go I didn't know if I could deal with this life

anymore

The saying "words can never hurt me" is untrue...

because they do

They cut deeper than a knife

It takes longer for those wounds to heal

I have no clue what to do

With no voice to be heard

I have no way to deal

Chapter Three

At A Glance

We moved to several different places

But it never seemed to work out

Dad kept getting locked up

Mom had to keep getting him out

This always created an issue

It's not like we had savings in the bank

Although he would come up with what was lost because of him

The fact that it happened in the first place

Never seemed to bother him

It didn't seem to occur to him that his arrest also affected us

Especially me

I had to sneak him cigarettes in jail

I met with a guy I didn't know to give him the contraband

To this day I fail to see why he chose me

I was confused to why he had to be in these streets

But he would always say "I'm the man of the house and I gotta do what I gotta do to take care of my family"

Although he was in the streets, he tried to have his own business

When he did work, he did it well

A whole lot better than being in and out of jail

I was the child that wrote up his contracts

While he was in those streets... I was put to work

Made every contract look good because

Greatness was expected of me

He set the bar really high...

A height I tried my best to meet

Through all the trials and tribulations

Through all the hurt and pain

I still wanted to put a smile on his face

Loved to hear all the kind words he would say

Some days were good and others were really bad

When the kind words went away

Those days made me sad

How could I go from "baby girl" to a hoe?

Being good for nothing anymore

The daily tongue-lashes were brutal to say the least

So many nights I cried myself to sleep

It would occur in rounds, from my mother, to my brother

Then my sisters and then me

How could he tell me in one breath that I have "aging beauty,"

And in another that no one would ever love me?

Would I not be loved because of the person he said I was gonna be?

Or was it because he really didn't love me?

I knew that he did, but sometimes it was hard to tell

Maybe it was the drugs...

He was under some kind of spell

Every day it was something different

I was ugly... I was stupid...

I was a no-good human being

I wondered if this was all true

Could this really be me?

I thought: he's my dad, so it must be true

He is supposed to know me... right

Maybe he sees something that I don't

He knew things about the older ones in the crew

So why wouldn't he know them about me

I was his baby girl, so why couldn't he see

I did everything in my power to make him proud of me

I could no longer stay at home when he would leave

I had to go with family

Family who was sick of seeing me

I was unable to rest in my own bed

I was unable to sit and clear my head

I asked my mother why he would never let me stay home

With no reason why from her I was left feeling empty

There was no way I could ask my dad

Questioning him was definitely not an option

Then one day it all came out

I then knew why he wouldn't leave me in the house

The truth was disgusting, horrifying

I couldn't even shed a single tear

I couldn't believe my own ears

Surely this was a joke?!

He couldn't believe this to be true

He was so adamant about his accusation

He said it multiple times as though he had proof

Proof that not only was his baby girl a hoe...

But a hoe that would sleep with her brother, too!

He would always apologize for the things that he said or did

It made things ok, until he had an episode again

My mother could do nothing right, it seemed

My brother was a lost cause

It was almost like he blended in with the trees

He never really stood out regarding anything

The oldest two only added fuel to the fire

Although both got married and moved away

Their problems and issues came back to stay

It seemed like they had never left

Because of their poor judgement and their bad decisions

I had to deal with his frustration in regards to how they

were living

I was always a part of the Before, During, and After

In the movie of their lives, I remained a part of the cast

He tried his best to help them through

Because of whatever he had gone through in his life

Regardless of the hell he dragged us through

He wanted the best life for his crew

But as history had shown and still ever-present

They were hard-headed and didn't want to be still

We took in kids from one

She was tired and needed a break

The other returned to us in shambles...

Her marriage was a huge mistake

So, in the midst of all I was dealing with came more storms

And they came really quick, with full force

Me still being hopelessly naive

I still wanted to see good in them

I still wanted to believe

Believe that they were the decent people that we were

raised to be

Believing the stories they told to me about their situations

Believing that they did nothing to be hurt

By the people they chose to have dealings with...

I soon had a revelation

My dad would always say "for every action, there's a reaction,"

You can't believe everything they say

I began to think back on how their situations began

And realized that it started out on its way to a bad end

Both were in abusive relationships

Both were cheaters too

One was so desperate for the attention of a man

There was nothing she wouldn't do

Always being the eye of a storm

With nowhere to go and no comforting arms

I had to find a way to release

Some way to let this all go...

I was so full of words I could not verbalize

They ran through my head every time I closed my eyes

I was unable to speak, so therefore I wrote

This way was my only way to release…

The only way I knew how to cope

I wasn't trusted to go anywhere

Though Dad had always said "I will trust you until

You give me a reason not to"

And I'd never given him a reason…

His distrust in me came from the reasons of others

No matter how good I was it wasn't good enough

Since I couldn't go and "hang out"

I threw myself into every school activity that I could

The only way that I could delay going home

Home is supposed to be a safe haven

But that wasn't the case for me

Home was Hell…

Although I became involved in what I thought

Constructive things

It wasn't enough, he still found ways to belittle me

Trusting me didn't seem to be an option for him

Their faults and their sins became mine

The youngest scorned due to the oldest

No matter what I did or didn't do

I could never get genuine trust from him

Whenever he came at me about things that I did

I sucked it up and dealt with it

I was still just a kid

But it seemed that I would always be accused of

doing the things that they did

Being a cheater, a liar, and even a hoe

Those were sins of the others... including my mother

Since that was their path then surely it would be mine

I don't have much time left

I'm so done with living this life

I was the last of four

So things should be much simpler, I would think

Well... I became the referee between him, her, and the

streets

We still moved around

Just not as frequently

The fights still occurred

But now they involved me

He would always have a talk with me after every battle

But now it was just me

I began to unravel

He would explain things to me

Things I was too young to hear

I couldn't say a word

Only shed silent tears

It felt like I had to pick sides

And I didn't know who to choose

Dad was open about his mess

But my mom would pick and choose

I felt sorry for her and all she'd endured

What was I to do when I felt like she wasn't telling the truth

I was only a kid

I had nothing to do with what the adults did

Although the others were grown and out of the house

Their lives intertwined with my own somehow

From taking care of their kids

To keeping an eye on the second oldest after

Multiple attempts at suicide

I was still being cursed out about all they did and didn't

do

I could always hear his words...

"I ain't gone take this shit from you!"

I never showed signs of rebellion

I did what I was told

I was a good girl...

A good student...

A good mother to those I didn't give birth to

But none of this seemed to matter

He never seemed to be moved

I was tired of it all

It felt like I was going insane

And none of the others checked in on me

It was like they had forgotten my name

Being the baby didn't mean a damn thang

Although I was coping with the pressure of basically being a mother

I also had to manage the normal-for-us ordeals

My mother was a cheater and I was in on it

I was doing my father wrong because

I knew what she was doing and didn't tell him

I'd heard these accusations so many times before

They were old and tired

I couldn't see where she had time

If she wasn't on her paying job

She was out driving him around so he

Could come up with some ends

This was a daily thing

As quickly as the money came in it went out just the same

So, I couldn't see how she could cheat

Where did she have the time for it?

He would repeatedly have her swear to God on our lives

But that didn't matter

He still told her she was a liar

He would try to explain his reasoning to me

But what could I do if he did convince me?

He told me a lot of things that I didn't care to learn

But what could I say, "Daddy these are things that

I'm not supposed to hear"

To reiterate, it wasn't an option to speak

So, I sat there attentive for hours on end

I didn't know what to think

She would only speak when he left and blamed

His actions on the streets

Again, I state: I was only a kid

I had no clue what to do

I just stayed in my room and hoped

The storm would blow through

Chapter Four

It's About Her

When I was young, me and Mom were really close

I was her baby and could do no wrong

I remember sitting at the table playing cards and dominoes

Just us two killing time and throwing back a few beers too

It was our little secret

No one else needed to know

This was our routine while the others were at school

It was awesome being the youngest child

I got to chill out and let go

It was all fun and games

She let me run outside barefoot after a hard rain

She had a little song that she would sing

And I would tiptoe down the street and sprint back to her

Just as happy as I could be

The storms hadn't started, or so it seemed

We were just one big happy family

Little did I know she was hiding it from me

She would go to work and come home

Every day appeared to be the same

She worked the late shift and I would stay up until she came

She would always call to check if I was asleep

But I would always answer the phone

Just to hear her tell me to go to sleep

I wouldn't and couldn't until she walked through the door

I don't know if it was really because of her

Or because we were always home alone

I saw her in the morning before school and not again

Until the following morning, if I'd gone to sleep

As soon as I heard her keys in the door, I would be out like a light

I didn't have to stay up anymore

When the first storm came (that I can remember)

She had to walk off her good job

She could barely hide the pain

That weekend trip landed her in an unfamiliar world

She held up as best as she could

She couldn't get a job because the culture was different

A southern bell in this northern atmosphere

She wouldn't have fit in…

She wouldn't have been able to handle business

Considering the circumstances, she did all she could do

Keeping us kids together while living in a "wild zoo"

She was just as scared as us, if not more

Maybe it was because she became used to the storms

She now speaks on how we had to barricade

Ourselves in a hotel room

Dad hadn't paid the bill yet, and she didn't know

If he would be back soon

She didn't know if he was out trying to make some

money

Or if he'd wound up in jail

Either way, mentally, she was in a constant Hell

She couldn't do anything but go along with whatever

Walking in the midst of storms because we had no shelter

I can't imagine how she must have felt

Not being able to do for your kids or even yourself

That's a mother's worst fear

Although she wasn't by herself

He was the bread-winner

Even though there wasn't much bread

I don't know if or how often she may have prayed

But it had to be a great deal

Since she's still here today

I can say that the consistency was there

The storms came one after another

Now the target was on my mother's back

I don't know if he was upset because these southern streets

Didn't carry the same "things" to feed his habit

But he took it out on her...

What seemed like every day

Nothing was good enough

No matter what she said or did

She would get tired... this much I know for sure

She even tried to leave once, when I was young

But that proved to be no good

We went to her mother Mimi's house to stay

That didn't last too long

Her mother took a brass-monkey figurine to her face

So, my dad came and got us

He was irate to say the least

I believe he was ready to shed blood

They had jumped on my mother

Our Mimi and our two youngest aunts

And they did it in front of her kids

He was good to my mom for a while after that

But all good things must come to an end

Although I'd already been through a lot

I thought that it was more than enough and

That it shouldn't be anymore

My life seemed like a natural disaster searching

For new territory to explore

If I felt this way, I couldn't even imagine how my mom

felt

She did her daily routine

Wake up, work, drive, clean, and sleep

She tried to enjoy every piece of any day that she

could...

Which was little

She didn't have very much alone time

Between working, dealing with four kids, and being

My dad's licensed driver

But what could she do

And where could she go

She was just like us... his kid

They were together for so long, and from such a young

age

He pretty much raised her

In the book of my mom's life, my dad was on every page

So honestly... what was it for her to do

He was all that she knew

She knew it was bad, but she didn't have anyone to turn to

She was always on the road with him

She knew nothing about the streets

But she was on them constantly because of him

And just like her, I was too

I knew situations that the other kids didn't

She held me close when we had to visit jail

To go to court, to take him drug paraphernalia

Or to add money to his books, or to bail him out

Either way it was scary as Hell

I never quite figured out, and still haven't till this very

day

Why was I always the kid to go while the others stayed?

I saw things, heard things, and even learned some

Things from being by her side

I learned how to suck it up

And keep a steady stride

When you have to take care of business

You show No Weakness

Things weren't as bad now, in my older age, as they were when I was younger

I mean, food was still scarce, but there weren't as many mouths to feed

She wasn't in the streets with my dad that much anymore

He was doing side jobs more now and was closer to home

And he was comfortable driving around town

But when she was home, she stayed behind closed doors

We shared words, but not a whole lot more

I guess when one thing leaves another takes its spot

So, the streets were replaced with grandkids

It was a revolving door

It was always something

I began to expect a new storm, not a light rain

When it came it always poured

It was a different face every time, but it had the same name

I didn't see how it was fair to her

Her "baby" was now venturing into high school

It was like they took turns

When one kid left, another came in

And even in these stories

I was on every page

When they both left to take care of business

The kids were left with me

So even if I was allowed to go anywhere, I couldn't

I had children to take care of

I didn't grumble and complain; I wouldn't dare

In many ways I was like her… TRAPPED

I could tell she had begun to change

And that she was also tired

But it doesn't really explain the events that transpired…

So, let's fast forward to my high-school junior year

The kids were no longer permanent residents in the home

But came quite often

Now it was down to three; him, her, and me

Things should be ok, right?

Well, think again

Every time a fight broke out

She would run to show me what he did

I cared... but also didn't...

I'd gotten used to it

I didn't want to see it again

I would still wonder why she didn't leave

She didn't have to wait until I graduated

I was older, I could work

We could make ends meet

She started to get on my nerves

We could leave and we would make it

She no longer had to sit here and take this

The job she had was with the school

So her schedule was set and we knew what she had to do

My dad was adamant about informing

Others in the household of changes in our schedule

I was still involved in sports and was allowed

To go to friends' houses

People I'd known forever

So, one day when school was over I did the same routine

The clock moved just the same

But something had changed

I knew that things came up that could alter a day

I didn't become alarmed until my dad came

As we already know, my dad moved around a lot

So, when he beat my mom home, didn't know where she was,

And hadn't heard from her

Both our hearts stopped

We drove around areas her job took her through

We called her mother who claimed she didn't know

She could have been in a ditch somewhere and nobody knew

This was unlike her

Neither of us had a clue what to do

That day became another and she was still gone

Went to her job and she was nowhere to be found

The day turned into night and we called her mom again

That's when our jaws hit the ground

They knew where she was

They helped her leave

And I got: "And I'm not gon' tell you where she is"

As she chuckled and hung up on me

Our worry turned into rage

I couldn't believe how they laughed

Like this was funny; fun and games

My mother had disappeared

And no one felt compelled to tell me where

I heard from her throughout the years

That when I graduated, she was going to leave

I heard that statement countless times in my ear

So now I was wondering what happened

This wasn't my senior year

I hadn't walked across that stage

So how dare she leave me

That wasn't part of the plan

This plan was her own and she neglected to inform me

But she could tell them

The same people who jumped on her in front of me

I didn't know why she did it now

And at this point in time, I didn't even care

Yes, I knew what she had been through... I was there

But she went about it the wrong way

And her people had the audacity to laugh in our face

I already knew how they felt about us

So I didn't really care if I had to pull every

Strand of hair out of their heads until they decided to share

I think the same thought crossed my dad's mind

He stated that he should "turn me

loose on them" for laughing the way that they did

Meaning, allowing me to go put my hands on them

For laughing in our face

It was blatant disrespect

Which was something we did not tolerate

Regardless of what they thought or felt about him

I was still her kid

That didn't matter to them nor her

And now it didn't matter to me

I wasn't important enough for her to tell me her plans

I don't recall when or how I fell asleep

But when I woke up the following day

Things were definitely different

I now see how relentless she could be

Days went by and she ran into my sister

She wanted her to get me to understand

Why she left the way she did

But there wasn't a good enough reason that she could give

I didn't want to look in her face

And I surely didn't want to hear any type of defense

She was gone, so let her stay gone. I was good

A lot of information came out while she was gone

He released a lot. He, too, was a person scorned

He was angry, worried, and also missed her

Love is a confusing thing

Not sure what happened to her while she was away

But for some reason she came back

The atmosphere was dismal and cold

I was happy she was ok

I was even relieved to see her

But that didn't subdue the fact that I now viewed her as a deceiver

Her handling of the situation would forever transform

our connection

She acted as if she was upset with me

She came back acting strange

Overly timid, as if she feared for her life

If that was true, then why did she come back

To the very thing that caused her to feel that way?

This was all too much for me to contend with

I had this foolishness damn near every day...

But I was leaving soon

And I couldn't wait to get away

My senior year finally came

Our interaction was the same

My words were limited

There wasn't much joking around going on

She would roll her eyes at me

Talk about me to her family

She forgot that when she cried, I cried

That bond couldn't get any deeper

Dad got locked up again and would remain there

Until after my graduation day

My mother told my brother not to waste his time

It wasn't much to see anyway

It seemed like she didn't care that I heard what she had said

I assume it was intention to get inside my head

So, a major milestone in my life had come and gone

And although my mother was there

I still felt alone

Friends from other schools came to see me

Sadly enough, that was the only thing that made me happy

I hoped that one day things between us would change

Certainly not like they were before she left; that I knew for sure

But when that change would occur was unforeseen

I was told by my dad: "love your mother

and respect her because you're supposed to, but you

don't have to like the things that she does"

So, I loved her and respected her as I should

I was supposed to be her baby girl

But that title was no longer any good

She was my mother

I guess she did the best she could

Chapter Five

It's About Him:

The Protector & Hustler

We were two peas in a pod

When it was just us two

Just me and my daddy

Our time together away from the house

When we would go fishing

At a young age I was always around him

And although I don't remember

The conversations we had, I knew there were many

He had a lesson to teach with every breath that he took

So, I have to assume that some of his words stuck

It was our time together that made our bond so tight

We would ride the bus to a gas station across town to pick pecans

I would always ask him to crack mine

Until the day he decided to show me how

One of many circumstances that he used

As a lesson to teach me

As he was showing me how to crack pecans, he quoted some words

That he said were from the Bible

"If you give a man a fish he will eat for a day, but if you teach him how to fish, he can eat every day"

That stuck with me

That was my daddy

He always had something smart to say

With him, there was never a dull day

He was my daddy and I was his baby girl

Just being in his presence made my entire world

Daddy rode around in a long Lincoln town car

He would come and go all the time

I had no idea that he was going so far

I was young, so I assumed when my dad wasn't home, he was at work

Looking back, he did stay gone a lot

But by my watch it was minutes instead of hours or days

All I know is when he was home, we were complete

He would bring us stock for our candy store

Teaching us about business early

He allowed us to sell the candy to the neighborhood kids

He would build a fire in the backyard so we could toast

Marshmallows and make s'mores

He would tell us stories by the fire

And always end with some type of lesson

We would do things like this and so much more

Never any harsh words coming out of his mouth

Life was good, you see

Mom…Dad…my siblings and me

All in the family…a happy family

Or so it seemed

It all changed during this supposed "vacation" he

had offered to take us on

We were excited to go at that time…

We were surely going to have fun

A road trip would be sweet

But that taste quickly became bitter once we arrived

This was no "vacation"

This would become our lives

At first, not knowing what this would be…We were

happy

There were so many sights to see

Then came reality

I had only seen him in "daddy mode"

A protector, provider, and nurturer

Making sure my got to work

Ensuring his kids had food and a safe place to sleep

This was the man that I knew

But there was another side to him

One that wasn't all that nurturing

I knew my daddy's name

But it was different in these new streets

He was different... even his speech

There were things that I didn't know about my own father

So regardless of the uncertain future I was to endure

It was intriguing to me...

I wanted to learn about this unfamiliar face

He was familiar with this northern atmosphere

With this culture that was new to us

He seemed to be comfortable in this environment that was

Scary and strange to us

There was another layer to who he was

A layer I wanted and needed to see

Who was this man?

And what was it that he could teach me?

No matter how hard it would be

I was determined to get to know the other side of my

daddy

Once the rain started, the storms

Came again and again

We were shaken but it didn't seem to faze him

I don't know if I should say that he was used to it

But it surely didn't break his stride

Regardless of how hard it got

He walked with confidence

This small thing became a valuable takeaway

No matter how hard it gets

You never let them see you sweat!

He would always say "You're not looking for nothing

on the ground, so hold your head up!"

And that's exactly what he did!

He kept his head held high

We never saw him sweat

In the midst of the storm this was a lesson I'd never

forget

Although things were awful

And there appeared to be nothing good coming our way

I still wanted to go where he went

I still enjoyed all the time that I spent with him

He still tried to create some form of family time

It wasn't as pleasurable as before

There was no backyard gathering

No brisk walk to the park

It was more like walking through a jungle full of savage beasts

That was the scenery every time we had to walk those streets

But to me, because I was with him, it was fine

I saw a little bit of my old dad in this other man

And because he was still there

I still enjoyed holding his hand

I would not show the fear inside of me

And honestly, what did I have to fear? Really

I had a superhero walking beside me

I would see things; things I probably shouldn't have seen

But every sight became a life lesson from him to me

There was nothing that occurred in this Hell we were in that he

Didn't turn into a teaching session

For as long as I can remember until recently

There wasn't anything I couldn't go to him about

There was always something that he could teach me

Spending all of this time in this cesspool of a city

Walking… riding… wondering… even sleeping in these streets

I saw a man who was unfamiliar to me

Saw that my dad had a hustler's mentality

This is why he was able to maintain in these streets

As this other man that none of us had got to meet

This was all normal to him

He was used to being in these streets

By the way he carried himself we would never have known

That this was his life when he was not at home

This was a life that he knew and knew all too well

Was that a good enough reason to drag his family

Into the middle of pure hell?

No security… no steady finances… very little food to eat

Was it really that important for him to be in these streets?

I stated I wanted to get to know this new man

Clearly, I got what I asked for

He was still my daddy... Superman to me

And I saw his kryptonite one night after everyone went to sleep

I didn't know what it was

It wasn't anything I'd ever seen

A needle and a spoon that was burnt on the back

This is when the truth about this man came out

My mother tried to explain what it meant

Why we were in these circumstances

Why Daddy didn't want to leave

Things that I had seen so innocently started

To become clear as my mind played it all back to me

He was in his natural element being in these streets

The dad I was used to showed up only when necessary

I can't say I was mad, hurt, or even disappointed

I didn't know what this stuff was

At that time, I didn't know what it could do

If I knew then what I know now I would have thrown a

fit every time

He met up with these different dudes in those streets

But he was still my dad, so what could I have said

I was still a child and couldn't comprehend

What was going on in his head

We never knew if he was alive or dead

Locked up or free

Anything could have happened to him out there in those streets

This was now our life and we tried to make do

You never know what you can handle in life

Until you actually go through it

It's nice to think that all good things remain the same

But I found out the hard way

That the game will always change

Some nights Dad came home and other nights he didn't

Going from bad to worse because he wasn't there

Who would handle these people, this environment?

Where would the money come from?

Even though we had hungry nights before

Somehow it was worse when he didn't come

Walking through the door

Not only were we starving, but terrified as well

There was no one to shield us from our current place in Hell

When he did walk through those doors it was still bad...

Just not terrifying

We knew he would protect us

He was the Man of Steel

It may not have appeared that way

But he knew exactly what dragons to slay

There were clear boundaries that were set

No one was to harm his family

Unless they wanted a bounty on their heads

All the days began to merge

None stood out more than the other

If every day is bad or worse

They all start to blend together

Regardless, he always found a way to make it work

Beit that he made sure we had a full course meal

Even if it was just for one day

Or making sure we had a warm place to stay

He was an adaptive and persuasive man

He could talk a person out of their last

Good or bad... hot or cold

He always found a way to make us whole

It seemed like time stood still

It didn't seem like the rain would ever stop

We were here and then over there

We were never up... always down

I'm surprised I didn't grow up with a permanent frown

Only he knew what was going on

Only he knew what was in the making

We didn't know when we were going home

He never had that conversation

But then that day did come

And he told us that we were going home

I don't know how he made it happen

But we were all so happy to leave this hellhole

We were getting out of this abandoned house

Where so many others would sleep

We no longer had to look over our shoulder

When we walked the streets

We were going back to a familiar place; a place of peace

We were going home and we all took a sigh of relief

When we flew back home, we were greeted by his

family

Things were going to be anew

We would have food to eat and a comfortable place to sleep

I would see my dad once more

Not the hustler I'd seen in those streets

Once again, we would go fishing by the creek

Life was going to be good again

No more bad days or worse

We would finally have something

My mom could go to work

We would now be able to go to school

No more wondering what we were going to do

We were around family that we knew

Kids our age

We didn't have to walk the streets anymore

All of the seclusion, hurt, pain

And hopelessness was left behind

Things could only go up, right...?

Life was going to get better for us... or so I thought

But my dad had still more sides that I had not yet seen

I knew the nurturer

I met the hustler... the man in the streets

Never would I have imagined that he could be so mean

I don't know where this man came from

But I didn't want to get to know him

I could deal with the hustler because of his devotion

This new one, I wasn't so sure of his motivation

Chapter Six

It's About Him, Part II:

The Abuser

All types of truths started to come out

Not long after our return home

It's difficult to come across information that's so personal

I was filled with all kinds of emotions

There was no one certain way to feel

Members of my own family didn't like me; didn't like kids

This was one truth that was told to us by our dad

But there was no way we could react

We had to deal with their ill treatment

We were under the same roof as them

All we could do – all we were allowed to do

Was hold it in and grin

Being disrespectful was not an option

As you know… he didn't raise us to be that way

There was no retaliation

There was no repeating what was said

It was just something that we knew

Something we kept in the back of our head

Couldn't understand then and still don't understand now

How can a child make you treat them so foul?

Where is this type of behavior even allowed?

We were taught that God deals with a person's heart

For that reason, we weren't allowed to play the foolish part

We were taught, so we knew better

We were expected to be better

One would think an eye for an eye... Right?

Maybe... But whose eyes are you looking through?

These things may have happened before my time

Maybe my mom just kept her mouth shut, thinking

It was all in the past

I don't know where this man came from

I just know he was outright mean

Was it our circumstances that made him act this way?

Or the fact that we came back

Meaning that his dealings in the streets had to change?

Regardless of the reason this man came to be

I didn't want to get to know him

This individual was not nurturing

This individual started knocking my mother to the floor

This guy was not my dad

This wasn't the person who used to take me fishing

His words were no longer building me – us – up

They was tearing us all down

In these moments of his madness

I didn't want him around

What was so different about now as opposed to before?

To my knowledge, he never raised his hand before

What happened for this to change?

Why did the protection and nurturing have to end?

Hopefully this was all temporary

This wasn't permanent

This guy wasn't here to stay

It was because of our circumstances

This would be over any day

Any day never came

This man decided that he wanted to stay

This person was going to wreak havoc in our lives

On many occasions we were awakened from our sleep

Yelling and screaming was all we heard

He was doing all of the talking

She barely said a word

A number of times we were awakened by

A hand being placed on our heads

He would make her swear on our lives

She had to swear that she was telling the truth

Telling the truth about what?

We had no clue

This episode was on repeat constantly

It didn't matter that we had to go to school the next morning

The only thing that mattered to him was the truth

What truth he was looking for?

I'm still unsure

He asked the same questions and made the same allegations

No matter how many times she swore

On our heads, on the Bible

It wasn't enough

He still didn't believe her

And because he didn't believe her

He became angry

That anger always made the situation worse

How much worse can worse get?

I didn't know, but as my dad would always say

"It doesn't take a psychic to look at the chain of events

and figure out what the outcome may be"

So, looking at this chain of events

What do you think the outcome will be?

It was a lot of back and forth

We would have our own place

And then we wouldn't

He would be nice and "put together"

Then be mean and ferocious

I didn't know which dad would show up from day to day

He was a strong, proud man

But there were some things about him that I didn't understand

How could he go crazy when someone else hurt us?

Yet here he was hurting us on the regular

Did he not know that he was hurting us too?

Was it a different kind of hurt to him, since he provided for us?

A host of unanswered questions festered inside of me

Here was my dad, my Superman

The apple of my eye, making his family cry

And to this very day I haven't figured out why

All of his wise words were followed by painful ones

He was so direct and serious when he delivered both

I could never tell if he was high or sober

What state of mind was he in when those words

Began and the others ended?

I don't know which is more painful...

The hurtful words

Or not knowing if he meant them or not

Although I was hurt, stunned, tearful, and torn

He was still my Superman and I still loved him dearly

All of the bad emotions were temporary for me

Somehow I would brush it off and move on

At least until the next time...

I can't even say if there was ever an apology

I don't know if he even remembered the mean things he said

Was he aware of the words that he spoke?

The things he said, no one else would be allowed to say

He would tell others not to speak down to his kids

And that we, his kids, couldn't call each other names

So why was it that he went against all this

And said the things that he said?

Who was this man that was supposed to shield us from the rain

But instead brought a hurricane?

"Sticks and stones may break my bones, but words will never hurt me" – that was a lie, he said

Although sticks and stones leave a visible bruise

That bruise can heal

So well that you would never know that it was even there

Words, however, hurt a lot longer

The pain is not temporary like that of a stick or a stone

Which is why you should be mindful of what you say to people

You can't say whatever you want to say and think it's ok

These words….

Words like these is why it was so hard to hold onto the hurt

He wasn't in his right mind…

How could he say these words

And yet have so many hurtful words to say?

I would have preferred the sticks and stones

Over his words any day

Those words that he spoke left bruises

That hurt me to my core

And considering how my siblings turned out

Apparently, those words damaged them too

I know that people are different

And they cope with things differently

But they heard the same advice that I heard from him

So, I'm not sure why we are all so far from his wisdom

They've allowed those mean words to manifest

And mold them into the people they are today

It's an excuse... It's a way to justify...

No one can predict what they may go through in life

No one can stop the challenges that may come their way

You can't run away or hide

You can, however, become a better person because of it...

In spite of it all

Yes, it's easier said than done

But it is indeed possible

Even if wise words didn't follow the hurtful ones

I would have had to find a way

I wish I could say that things got better as time went on

But they didn't

Mom was still getting cursed out and hit

Dad was still in the streets

And here I was trying to hold my peace

My dad would always say

"There's a thin line between sane and insane"

I didn't know which side to place my feet

I couldn't very well go insane

I now had kids to keep

Through it all, I believe he started to forget

That I was still a kid

Maybe that would explain what he did…

It was another typical day

I went to school

Mom went to work

He was running the streets

I don't know if any words were exchanged

Between my parents that day

Either good words or bad

Did the chain of events that occurred that night

Spill over from earlier in the day?

All I do know is that my feelings changed

I actually was upset with my dad

These feelings weren't short-lived

Unlike before

Everything else that he did or said, I got over it quickly

But this time was different

This time something changed

I no longer felt like Daddy's little girl

I just remember hearing my dad storming through the door

And heading straight for my mom in a fit of rage

And hit her

I jumped out my bed and ran to the living room

And that's when everything changed

My dad, my Superman, my protector, looked at me

In the most deranged way

Anger was looking at me and asked

"What you gonna do?!"

And just like that...

This man swung at me

Caught the lower half of my face

It would have been worse if it weren't for my reflexes

And the pain of my heart minimized the pain of my face

I was speechless, too hurt to even cry

He tried to apologize later

Promising things he couldn't afford to make it up to me

But it didn't matter

All I could say was "Yes, sir"

I couldn't express my hurt and disappointment

So I did the only thing that I could do

I stayed silent

I held it in and moved on

And it wasn't because I wanted to

It was because there were no other options

Only he was allowed to show that he was upset

Even though I know my mom couldn't defend me

I still wonder why she didn't try

The closeness that I felt with my dad

Didn't feel so close anymore

Chapter Seven

It's About Him, Part III:

The Man & His Addiction

Out of all of his kids he confided in me

He explained the reasoning behind many of

His actions, his circumstances…

His methodology

He told me things that hadn't been spoken to any other

He never forewarned me about these discussions

They came in the midst of other topics

Like they were examples to explain the topics at hand

Maybe he needed to let it out

Maybe he wanted to explain his actions

Maybe he thought that out of all of his kids

I was the only one that could handle it

Believe it or even understand it

A lot of things came out that I wasn't ready to receive

Things that I probably shouldn't have heard

Still, I listened every time he decided to release

I don't know if it was hard or easy for him to do

I appreciate that fact that he allowed me

To get to know the man that he was or wanted to be

I got to see the man behind the madness

I was able to hear why certain situations played out

The way that they did

They say that there's always two sides to a story

I only heard... saw... lived one side

Now I got to hear the other side: his side

Situations and experiences way before my time

Things he endured through childhood until now

His release also released me as well

I understood some of the things that he did

Missing pieces of the puzzle were put into place

The story made sense now

He wasn't the only one to blame

The same face using a different name

My dad was firm about allowing us around people

He didn't care if it was family members or people from school

"If you spend enough time with someone

their ways will rub off on you and you won't even know it"

He took offense when we would call someone our friend

A person we only speak with in school

Someone we joked around with

Anytime we would say "my friend"

He would correct us

One day he told me that the title "friend" you

Can't give to just anybody

That's something that has to be earned

He went on and stated that he didn't have any friends

He knew a lot of people, but they were not his friends

I thought it was sad that he felt that way

And then he told me why he felt the way that he did

There was once an individual that he called his friend

His best friend, or so he thought

He found out that his "best friend" slept with the mother of his kids

The one in which he shared four with

I could see the disappointment and anger in his face

He couldn't believe this guy could do that to him

He didn't want to be vulnerable like that again

Hurt by two people that he was supposed to be close to

So to save us, his kids, from the same kind of pain

He shielded us from the no-good people in this world

Although he tried to raise us to be good and kind

That didn't mean that others were trying to do the same

I understand why he wanted us to be mindful of

Who we gave that title to

I understand why I held on to that very principle

Everybody is not your friend

Every person you encounter will not value you

In the same manner as you

It's a word that is supposed to be used for people that you know…

Right?

Well, to me, it's a word that's supposed to be earned

Over time, through the good and bad

Is this person worthy of this title?

I know what kind of friend I would be

But I can only speak for myself

Will that person return the same loyalty, support, and consistency?

Can I trust them to be truthful?

Will they look out for my well-being the same way

They would look out for their own?

This is what I took from his side of the story

Because of him, I learned this principle

And just like him I stand firm on it too

"If you don't stand for something, you'll fall for anything"

He would say this in relation to almost everything

You can't live life going along with the crowd

If you don't know what you think or how you feel

About something or someone...

How would anyone else know

If someone makes a statement and you disagree with it

Then speak up

But in speaking up, it had to be fact

He was never big on us saying things that made no sense

Or making statements based on emotions only

You had to be able to show proof; a pattern of behavior

And with him that was hard to do

You had to take a stand

Meaning you had to defend your position to him and his words

I did speak up for myself on some occasions

He would say things about me that were just wrong

I would be accused of things based on the actions of my older siblings

He would say things that were so outlandish

That I couldn't hold it in any longer

And when I would speak up for myself

He would get happy

He would say "That's what I've been waiting on you to do!

If I'm wrong then tell me. How will I know that I'm wrong

if you don't speak up?"

In his very own strange way

He taught me a lesson

It's funny how my dad could turn anything into a teaching opportunity

He once spoke on the trees blowing in the wind

This was a conversation about a higher power that moves us

Even though we can't see it

Different things that came on television or certain

Songs that played on the radio

I remember him hearing the intro to a song by the 69 Boyz and

Turned that into a life lesson

About how some guys will say anything to get what they want

He will tell you you're pretty

He will say that you're the only one and that you are smart

He will even tell you that he loves you if it will make you feel good

The purpose of all these words is to one end

That result is the guy getting you in bed

So he was telling his baby girl

Not to let a guy fool her into thinking that he

Liked her or that he cares

"He just trying to say the right things to get into your head and get

you into bed. So don't be fooled, sweetie, he only wants one thing."

Please believe me when I say that my dad can turn anything into a life lesson

And I am grateful that he did

Although I wasn't allowed to socialize with boys

At least not in front of him

He always seemed to find a way to get on the topic of relationships

He would speak about all the things a man didn't

Like for his woman to do

The type of woman a man was looking for

What attributes were most appealing to a man

And, as usual, it was like he was reading my mind

He would always say how it was different if a male did something

Than if a female did something

That's just how it is...

For whatever reason, things are more acceptable from men, it seems

Although I don't agree with it

I've grown to see that it's true

The world has double standards

My dad used many analogies

This is the main one he would use to clarify why I should

"Carry myself" in a respectable manner

"You can't do what a man do! A man can go out here and sleep with fifty women and everybody knows it, but he can put on a suit and walk into a place and still be treated with respect. A woman, on the other hand, can sleep with only a few and her name will be put on every gatepost in town. She can put on a million-dollar dress and all they will see is a hoe!"

He said that to say this…

A woman's past can affect her future

No matter how well you dress up trash, it's still trash

And, as he stated, trash attracts flies

Honey attracts honeybees

Another one of his sayings

So, if you carried yourself or dressed trashy

You would attract a trashy man

If you carried yourself in a respectable way

You had a better chance of attracting a halfway decent man

However much I wanted to disagree with what he said –
because it

Wasn't fair for women to be judged and men not – it was true

I found that truth out before I entered the dating world

You can learn from other people's mistakes

Although he used a lot of analogies to explain things

He would always follow up with real-life examples

Things he had experienced throughout his life's journey

These examples made it real to me because

They were so close to home

So many words... so many lessons

He repeated himself constantly

I guess he knew that a person has to hear something

multiple times

Before it will be remembered

However long it was and however often

I now have an appreciation for every wise word he ever

spoke

In the midst of every storm, he always made it his

Business to talk us through it

Regardless of if we wanted to hear it or not, he would

speak those

Words, teach those lessons, and give those life

examples

There was more to my dad than his circumstances

There was more to him than his madness or harsh

words

In his words of wisdom...

In his hours of sanity...

In his release...

I found the man behind the addiction

Chapter Eight

Mental Note

I need to have a plan

I need to have my life together

There's no way in hell I wanna grow up and live like this

This life can't be normal

There's no reason that it should be this hard

I must do whatever possible to make sure I don't end up living this way

I'm already on the edge

I will make better choices

Surely it can't be that difficult

But I refuse to repeat the same pattern

I need to develop a plan

I need to write my plan down

So I don't forget it

So I can stick to it

Things will be different when I grow up

I refuse to live this way

Note to self... Don't become an addict

No one thing should be that important to you

My dad said "don't form a habit that you can't afford"

Yes, I'm sure he was talking about drugs, but that goes for anything

I don't want or need to be addicted to anything

I don't see the purpose

I really don't understand what people get out of it

Giving up your money...

Possibly giving up your family...

Your freedom...

And for what?!

A moment of euphoria

How long does this short-lived feeling last?

Not long – the reason to repeat the experience in the first place

How can something become so important to a person?

I can't understand it right now

Being the youngest of his kids that lived under one roof...

I saw a lot

I saw my siblings running from truth

I saw them fighting against what was right

I saw them picking up every bad tendency from

People they were around

I saw how they seemingly enjoyed it, too

True, we weren't allowed to do much

And yes, my daddy had "ground rules"

But they weren't all that bad

I thought they were reasonable

He always explained why these rules were in place

And why we should follow them

I never understood why they made it seem so bad

I heard him say again and again

"I will trust you until you give me a reason not to"

But for whatever reason they chose to give him a reason not to

Then acted out even more or complained when they

were disciplined

They would always say that I was the baby, so I got my way

This statement was far from the truth

I tried to follow the rules

I didn't see what was so fun or great "out there"

What was it that they felt they were missing out on?

Our life should have shown them

How hard it was "out there"...

Even though it was hell "in here"

They were trying to become everything he didn't want us to be

They did everything to break his trust in them

In their inability to do right and make good choices

So why were they shocked or hurt when he stopped believing

Things that they said?

Although I hadn't done anything to lose his trust... I inherently did

I suffered the repercussions of their actions and their

bad choices

So, while they were causing problems and trying to get away

I was left to deal with the aftermath

Therefore, when I grow up and have kids

I won't blame one for the other's actions

I will trust them separately, not collectively

The hands of one will not be the hands of all

To each their own

I will try and save them from suffering

Or being held accountable for someone else's actions

I will trust you until you give me a reason not to

Note to self: Don't call them names!

I know he loves me; he's my dad

He's there to protect me

He wasn't supposed to make me sad

All the name-calling screamed louder than anything

I could never figure out why he would get so mean

His actions would contradict his intentions

We couldn't call each other names

We couldn't pick on one another

I couldn't say "shut up, stupid"

Or get mad and say "wit yo ugly self"

He would chastise us for those seemingly harmless words

Calling each other names is what siblings do

What was the issue?

What was the big deal?

We were kids; that's what kids do… right?

This very thought was so very wrong

He would remind us that words are not harmless

I will adopt this principle as well

I will practice the same belief one day

I just won't follow up in the same way

I will not call mine names

Family does not call each other names

If I want them to follow this rule, then I must do the same

Follow the plan that you have laid out

Try to keep things in order

Don't stray too far out

If you keep your eyes on the prize

Then it shouldn't be that hard

Set a time limit to reach each goal

If you stick to this timeline, you should have

Everything in order before you get old

Guidelines, borders, boundaries, limits, and organization

are key

If I follow through with the plan everything should work

out for me

Yes, situations will arise

But I will be better equipped

He would always tell me that

"The world will beat you down, because that is what we

know

for sure. God never said it wouldn't be hard. And

although you may fall

down, that doesn't mean you're supposed to stay there.

Whatever you do never let the world harden your heart"

So, keep all this in mind and hold on to it

Everything will work out if you do

He, my future spouse, has to be better than it all

Better than all the chaos and noise that lives within

He has to understand my background and accept it

He will be into education as much as me

Structure is the key

I should be able to share without fear of judgement

My mom would say "you can't tell a man everything, because he will

throw it back in your face"

I didn't want this to be true

Don't hide things… be transparent

Most of her issues arose from that thought process

I don't want to think that way

He will know all of me and love me still… won't he?

We will be friends above all

Friends don't get mad with each other

Friends can share everything

Friends accept you for who you are… they never judge

If that is present and solid, then all else should fall into place

If I stick to finding someone that fits this description

I won't go through what she went through

Never forget who you are and where you came from

As rough and unpleasant as it was – is – keep it

Hold on to all the hell and live better because of it

Carry the bruises

Hold on to the hurt

Use none of it as an excuse

This hell of a life doesn't make it ok to bring hell to another

I saw this life becoming an excuse for my siblings and their actions

This life should make you want to be better

I've seen and dealt with way too much at this age to cause anyone else

To feel what I have felt

I don't understand how they could

I saw what my dad put my mom through

I was learning what my mom had put my dad through

I refuse to take anyone else through the same

Will it be difficult for me?

I'm sure it will be; but who knows

My dad told us – me – "You have ways about yourself that will come naturally. Those are not good ways! You will have to work on it daily to keep yourself from acting that way."

I will work on it daily!

I will hear his words and try to catch myself when I'm

Visiting that familiar place

As long as I make a conscious effort, I should be ok

Hopefully...

Chapter Nine

I'm Confused

I have my plans... my goals

I'm working towards them

I am following my timeline

It's good to start strong

As long as you stay focused, all this other stuff shouldn't interfere

I can see the silver lining in this dark place

Things are going to be better

I'm on the right path at a steady pace...

                                            or so I was thinking

In my head I was building my future

Going about it in the right way

But as usual, the storm clouds came

They never stay gone for too long

It never fails

Every time the sun tries to peek through

The rain seems to come back

I don't understand

I'm confused at it all

How can he be mad that I did not fall?

I was still under their roof, but I wanted my own

I worked at good companies

Trying to make myself some money

I also wanted to help out

I can recall him saying to me

"I don't care how good of a man he is... a man will act funny about his

money, so make sure you have your own."

And while my dad was a good man

He acted funny about his money, when he had it

So therefore, I wanted my own

I didn't like asking for things

On the occasions when I did ask for things that I needed

I was met with harsh words

So I became guarded about asking people,

My people, for things

I only sought things that I needed, never anything that I wanted

So, I would work

And somehow, some way, that too was an issue

I had to find rides or wait for a ride

I was always being asked for money for his habits

I couldn't speak up for myself

And I knew no one else would speak up on my behalf

I was trying to do the right thing here

I would be less of a burden

But it appeared that me having an income was becoming

A burden all in itself

I thought that things would get better... easier...

A little more bearable

But this was a grave misconception on my part

I saw more troubling things

And I witnessed them all by myself

There was a little of the usual

Then came the new

I began to see what he was saying

"Y'all were better off going through hell with me than you would have been if I left you with your mother"

I'm compelled to believe that statement

How could a person treat a child that way?

How could she do what she did and look them in

The face the next day?

How could you strike a toddler with the full might of

your fist?

How could you kick a kid clear across half the room

And see nothing wrong with it?

How could a conscience allow a person to act in such

disarray?

Although they weren't my kids

I tried to protect them anyway

More and more burdens placed on my shoulders

This mess was messing with my goals

I had to delay or detour my plans

Because of others' plans, I was cast as the "helping

hand"

This was not a part of my design

In so many words or ways I became a "parent"

I didn't do, didn't go, didn't spend because of them

I was sacrificing for the young and the old

Apparently, a story had been written

One I am yet to have been told

I worked and went to school

Despite the hurdles that crowded my way

I walked myself into a storm

But I refused to let it lead me astray

So, I pressed on

The more I pressed the more resistance came my way

Although I now had my own issues

Somehow theirs were still in my face

I had no clue what to do

There were no words for how I was feeling in this space

Dad was still having encounters with the law

Words were still very limited with my mom

My siblings kept facing various struggles

And as usual, they needed my dad's assistance

Here I was, still in the midst of it all

And still the youngest...

At least I was supposed to be

But, as usual, I was the search and rescue team

In my personal storm and I stood in that rain alone

Their life was just that and they had no time

For anyone or anything else that was going on

Why was I going through this on my own?

I was facing jail time

And I felt like my dad's biggest concern

Was the money I was going to have to spend

I assumed he felt it would limit what I would give to him

All sort of questions went through my head

A lot of WHYs and WHATs and HOWs

But this was my bad choice... right?

I had to deal with it

No one else could sort this out

But my parents sorted it out for them!

I was baffled by how my dad showed up for all of them...

He made an appearance repeatedly

So why not show up for me, Daddy?

My dad would always say that

"If you put yourself in a bad situation, there can

only be a bad outcome"

So, this bad choice that I made put me in a

Bad situation, therefore resulting in a bad outcome

It was just a package I allowed a guy to mail to my house

I asked myself, How can you be mad

Or sad that you suffered through this alone?

This is no one else's fault but your own

So, however wronged I may have felt

I had to get over it and help myself

Disregard the fact that I'd been there for everybody else

This was your choice, I told myself, your fault, and there

is no need in you looking for anyone else

So, I stopped looking and kept trying to stick to the plan

I had no clue how this was going to turn out, but I had

to stay focused

Even when I was suffering in silence

No words on how I felt were spoken or shouted

I just wrote it out

I couldn't fathom how I ended up in this situation

I was in fear of my future

Or if I would even have one now

I guess all the planning and organizing didn't do much at all

I was stumbling and there was no one to keep me from falling

Was this my life?

Trying to make an easy dollar is never really easy

Although I tried to keep going

The same stuff continued to pull me back

The void of not having enough

The delusion that I wasn't supposed to make it

There was always the "new" that came to attack

I had no clue what to do

I don't even know how I got to this place... Or do I?

Maybe it's a truth that I don't want to face

My thinking was warped because of the things I'd gone through

I came to expect certain outcomes because of my upbringing

Although I wanted to do better and be better

Sometimes I would let my guard down and allow

Dark thoughts to roam around in my head

Running in those streets with dad had me thinking I was bad

I could handle whatever came my way

I also expected to end up in jail one day

It's not something that I wanted, it's just what I always thought

Something minor, like shoplifting, and I just got caught

At no time did I think

That I would be looking at 15 years for trafficking drugs

Foolishly agreeing to accept a package for some guy I barely knew

But he seen a stupid girl who thought she knew what she was doing

Remember, I was bad and used to dealing with the streets

I quickly realized that I was just used to walking through those streets

And, needless to say, this path that I chose didn't turn out well

Instead of our regular postal carrier

It was an undercover cop that rang the doorbell

This was my bad choice. I weathered my storm all alone

Arrest, roll calls, courts, jail, probation, and restitution

It was growing pains that I could have gone without feeling

But it made me realize that I need not allow bad thoughts to linger

And that jail is not for me

In many ways I was still naive

Chapter Ten

It's Not About Me Now

One bad choice shouldn't define me

It shouldn't stop me from achieving my destiny

Oddly enough, I wanted to be a lawyer

I plead to a lesser charge that could eventually be expunged

This is just a detour... that's all

I can still accomplish my goals

The charge is not even that serious

I can still do this

I'm going to continue on with my plan

Yes, I screwed up, but I will continue to stand

I don't have a choice

I can't live the way I grew up

I don't want to go through that for the rest of my life

I won't make it...

And because of 'that' I refuse to let 'this' keep me down...

I refuse to be beaten

I'm thinking positive

I'm moving forward

Things are going to be ok

I've completed my Associates Degree at technical school

And now I'm transferring to the school of my choice

Yes, things were scary

I was afraid that my negative background would hinder

my efforts

Nevertheless, the plan is coming together

Or so it seemed

I was moving forward

I was keeping my eyes on the prize

Despite the detour

I was trying to get back on track

But as usual, here comes something else

There's always something else!

It's just this 'something else' wasn't

Going anywhere EVER

As I was putting my plans into motion

As I was almost done with probation

The consequences of this awful choice I made

As I thought I was seeing a glimmer of light at the end of the tunnel

It went dark again

I know people are usually happy and it's something to celebrate

But I didn't share those same sentiments

I was upset… I was in disbelief… I was disappointed

I was hurt and I was mad at myself

My plans were being altered again!

I was trying to move on

Move forward

I wanted to experience life

A normal life

I wanted not to deal with

"It"… "stuff"… "things"…

I'm always dealing

I just wanted uncomplicated

I wasn't talking to my mom

My dad was actually serving time

So how in the hell was I supposed to handle this mess

without him

Without his guidance

Without his help

Here again I was out here on my own

Somehow, some way he was always there for my

siblings

And now he can't be here for me

So, among other things that I had to deal with

I had to accept the fact that this detour was life-altering

Everything changes

I'm no longer dealing with my sibling's kids

I now have to deal with my own...

I'm pregnant

It's no longer about me

It's about this person growing inside of me

This might sound crazy; will sound crazy

But I thought: this is about business

I don't have time to cry or feel sorry for myself

No, I'm not prepared for this, as I had planned to be

No, I'm not totally finished with my education

As I had hoped to be before something like this happened

But it is mine and if I struggle

I will do it on my own

I refuse to send it away because I'm tired and need a break

I refuse to send it off because I'm not ready to grow up and be a parent

I cannot and will not put my selfish needs first

In my mind I no longer exist

I don't have any wants

Anything that I do or don't do will be for the betterment of my child

I need to adjust my plans

Change my goals to include this new life

What I want is no longer important

What I need to do is all that matters

And the "need to do" is difficult enough

Without past occurrences making it more difficult to obtain

I know it is there inside of me and even though I can't even feel it yet

I'm feeling it…

I feel the pressure

I feel the consequences of my actions hurting it already

Because I am limited in what I can do to properly provide

How am I supposed to do this?

All I know is that I have to try

Before I got the news I was in the process of parting

Ways with this dude, Tim

Now I have to rethink some things

Eventually I will have to wear a ring

I have to create a family for this life growing inside of me

Although Tim wasn't a part of my future plans

I wanted to end it... both "ITs"

But there was no good enough reason for me to

Do either and be ok with it

And so it started...

Making choices in the best interests of the life growing inside of me

It wasn't that hard to stay with this dude

It was just the fact that he didn't fit in my plans

Tim had no drive, no need to grow, no goal to achieve

He wanted to play house and just be

The simplicity of his existence disgusted me

But I am with child now

We are young and surely he can grow

So, I thought, I can do this...

I can stay and create this family unit

A healthy family unit

Some things will be delayed

But I can still do this... right??

You'd think it would be a joyous occasion to share

This so-called good news with others...

I had to tell my mom, who I had no words for, that I was

with child

Over a year had passed since we had spoken

She was so excited to hear the news

I was disgusted with her reaction

How could she be so happy considering her prior

attitude and actions?

I wanted to hit her

She didn't seem to consider my situation... my plans...

my goals

She was just happy I was knocked-up by this boy

Why would she care if I was educated?

Why would she care if I had a job or not?

Why did I even expect her to?

It was not about me

The news was out about my pregnancy

Everybody had opinions and advice

But none really understood my sacrifice

People thought I was going to stay home

Not go away to school

And their truths about what, why

Or how I should do things in my situation

Motivated me to take that extended vacation

I was not about to deal with these people's

Rendition about how to raise my child

After all, I'd been doing this for a while

I was already readjusting my schedule

I was already, pretty much, taking a kid wherever I went

So, continuing to do this didn't mean shit!

At least this one is mine and I was doing it

For me. Well, for this kid

So, there was no real change, I thought, I got this

I'm leaving and that's it!

Yes, I will be alone

Yes, I will be away from people who can help...

supposedly

Yes, I will be in an unfamiliar city

But I made this kid...

It's my responsibility, not theirs

I'm giving up my life, not them

If I struggle, I struggle

If I get tired, then I will just be tired

If I fail, then I fail because of me and not because what was told to me

If I rise or fall it will be all on me

The choice to keep this kid is mine and mine alone

And, therefore, I will raise it on my own

Chapter Eleven

What About the Baby?

Now it was time to figure out my game plan

I made the choice to keep this kid

I also made choices because of this kid

Were they good or bad choices, I honestly didn't know

What I did know was that my tolerance level was no more

I decided to stay with Tim because of this kid

He needs to set some type of reachable goals

Not sure if he understands, as I do, that his life is no longer his own

Sacrifices are necessary…

Play time is over…

The time for trying to find one's self has halted

Like it or not this kid is coming and it will be

Depending on us for everything

As this kid grew inside of me

All I could think about was what was best for the baby

I ate things I never would have eaten

I was like Popeye eating spinach

Because of the baby

Everything I did was for the baby... our baby

But I was the only one thinking, doing, planning for the baby

This dude went about his business as usual

Yes, I can understand that nothing on his end would change physically

But I thought at least his mindset would have

He was still acting like some high-schooler

No plan... no projected goals...

No aspirations for anything

I began to notice just how dependent he was

On other people; his parents' guidance

It seemed like he was incapable of truly thinking for himself

Well, at least about important things

He was very capable of hanging out and getting high

Trivial matters were his area of expertise

The job he now had was because of me

The roof over his head was because of me

The car Tim now paid for was because of his dad

His dad knew the loan manager that financed the car

And the insurance on that car was because of me

So now I was wondering what in the hell I done got myself into

I was all for growing with a person and figuring things out

Trial and error… Yes, it is necessary

But only when you got the damn time

And there was no time, here! I thought

We gotta get things situated before this kid gets here

And that's not looking like a priority to this useless being

With the image of a family unit in place for this kid, I held on to hope

Hope that things would work themselves out

I told myself that I was just being overbearing...

I was anxious to still move away

I still had plans of going to school after the baby was born

A decent life could still be made

Yeah, I still had this predicament from that bad choice

Hanging over my head

And that also created anxiety for me

That anxiety pushed me to push Tim to try and do better

Was that right or wrong? I had no clue

But in my mind, it was necessary

It was necessary for him to understand that a life

Was going to be depending on him

Hell... two lives, to be honest

It would be me and the baby he had to care for

Finding a job would be impossible for me with a baby and a charge

That truth was harder for me to swallow than anything else

All was well with the pregnancy

The baby was healthy and on schedule with the medical growth charts

I was doing right by this kid, so far

And now I knew this kid was my son

I was happy… better yet, relieved

I was nowhere near girly, and it would have been a

Devastating blow to be told "it's a girl"

Personal preference… YES

I would not have known what to do

Even though, in my mind, a boy was best for me

It raised questions about Tim's ability

To actually show his son how to be a man when he is not

More apprehension piled on!

Now I was more eager than ever to push this guy to do right…

To modify his behavior and his mind

But this modification wasn't going well

This guy wasn't trying to plan for anything

I was the one suggesting moves to be made

I suggested the transfer of his job

I was the one who told him that was an option

And yet he seemed to complain about it all

He acted as if he was being forced to do things

Things that we had already agreed upon

The fact of the phone (that was in my name)

That I paid for monthly

Was more of a "look what I got" mentality

Than a "this is what is needed" mentality

It was needed to keep in touch with his pregnant lady

It was needed for business contacts from out of town

It surely wasn't needed for other females to be

Calling and leaving messages for him

It became clearer why his act wasn't coming together

I made the choice to have my son

He made the choice to be a "no good"

Here I was, again, with these irrational, unconventional

Emotions or reactions of mine

I wasn't hurt; I was livid!

I was pissed that I made a detour to have this kid

I was pissed that I was the only one

Willing to give up their entire life

I was disgusted that he wasn't man enough to speak

His truth from the start

If he had, none of this would be happening

His parents were trying to calm me down

I was looking for him and I couldn't find him

In the middle of the night

Having all kinds of pains

Having all kinds of thoughts and doubts

Eyes full of tears

This was not what I was expecting while expecting

I got on the road and went out of town that night

I headed to my oldest siblings house

She lived less than two hours away

I don't know what I thought that would accomplish

I don't know what I thought would happen if I didn't go

I thought I didn't have any other choice

This dude just messed up our lives

I guess I believed him because I had to

He called with an explanation about the voice mail

His parents had relayed my message, my visit, my disgust, my rage

What he said could have been true

The message could have been for his brother

This female could have been calling his brother "baby"

After all, no name was spoken

This pregnancy was too far along for me to try and prove otherwise

My son had to know who his dad is

Once again… it was about the baby

So, I spoke of it no more

But the phone I paid for would not be used anymore

I would have him involved because of this child

The love was lost and the trust was gone

But I would not raise this child on my own

I'm over it, I thought, I'm fine

I'm aware that my life is no longer mine

So, I will deal with him for the sake of my son

It's funny how life presents itself to you

It's amazing what your eyes allow you to see…

What your brain allows you to process…

What God removes from your reality

As I was sitting outside Tim's workplace

Not really sure why I was there

I saw him walking out with this girl

Friendly conversation from what I could see

As I drove across the parking lot to his car

As I looked at him and her

I thought I saw them holding hands

I thought they were walking a little too close for

coworkers

Could this be who left that phone message a while ago?

As I felt myself quickly escalating to a stage of

Pure concentrated rage… I blinked

It seemed longer than a regular blink of an eye

And when my eyes opened all thoughts were gone

He noticed that I was there, and they went their

separate ways

I didn't even ask him about her

I made a few remarks and left

Unsure if it was what I wanted to say

I guess that intercession was on behalf of my son

From My Father up above

Things seemed hopeful as we prepared to move

Since this pregnancy "me" turned into "we"

Tim's job transfer went through

And I managed to find employment too

There was still a great amount of reluctance on the

Family front about the move

One of my people flat out told him, "If you hurt her, I

will find you"

This person means exactly what they say

That may have been the reason why I held on to

The things that lay ahead

So, we moved...

Not too far bur surely far enough

I could drive back home in under two hours if things got

rough

Getting adjusted to a new environment

Getting familiar with the new terrain

It appeared that things were going to work out

Was I finally coming from out of the rain?

Was this the beginning of the family unit I desired without the pain?

Chapter Twelve

A Light Drizzle, Part I

Things were coming along after the move

My job wasn't too strenuous for my condition

It allowed me to help out with a few bills

And made me feel like things were going to work out

It was getting close to the time for my son to be born

So, there was more planning than ever before

What is it that I have to do…?

What is it that I need to do…?

What is it that I haven't done…?

The kid was about to be here soon

I had to make sure I had done all that needed doing

So here, yet again, there was no time for emotions

Even excitement or plain joy

It was all business, and my mind had no time for noise

It's sad to say that I considered those feelings to be noise

After all, I was on my own

My words of wisdom, my pillar of strength

My superman still wasn't home

I sometimes wonder if certain events in your life

Are a sign to stop what you're doing

Letting you know that you are not ready for whatever it

Is that you are about to do

The concept of taking care of a child was not hard to

grasp

I'd done it before

But the truth of carrying a child

Then giving birth was a dark area

I had no clue what to expect

What to look for

What to do or even when to do it

Many times I experienced contractions

But I didn't know it until after a conversation

With my oldest sibling

I would just manage and push through the pain

Well, the pushing through was soon to transition to

pushing out

While at work I felt constant pain and pressure

I would sit down for a while until it passed

Then go back to work

I was sitting down a lot one day

So I called my sister and told her what was going on

After she finished fussing at me for even being at work

So close to my due date

And waiting so long before calling her

She told me that I was in labor

Time was up, my son was on his way

Not sure I'm ready for this day

I called Tim and told him to head to our home

Town because I was having contractions; possibly in labor

A snowstorm was coming, uncommon for this area

Tim made it back to our hometown

We went to his parents' house

A few hours went by after our arrival

Weather alerts were all over the news

A snow storm was coming through

I began to panic, not wanting a home birth with emergency services

Snowed in and unable to get to me

So, I did the only thing I could do... I lied

I called my doctor and told him I hadn't felt the baby move in six hours

Although he was kicking me as I spoke

My doctor told me to head to the hospital

Thankfully he was on call for the local hospital

I didn't have to explain myself to anyone else

He examined me and said he had bad news

I hadn't dilated enough for him to admit me

Naturally, I threw a toddler fit

I refused to leave and told him he better handle it

And he did....

He manually dilated me from two to three centimeters

The pain shot through me like lightening striking a tree

On one hand I threatened to get him

And on the other hand I thanked him for not making me leave

The drugs were good and I was out like a light

I only woke to the doctor telling me it was time

Confused, I asked time for what?

As he chuckled he said it was time for me to give birth

My son was born without a hitch

He's here now and my gears had permanently switched

I was no longer auntie filling a mother's role

I was now a mother of my own

After leaving the hospital we had to stay in town

For a few days for follow-ups

Tim's parents offered us a room

Those few days seemed like years

Tim's mom stayed in my ears

I couldn't wait to go back to my place

Where I didn't have to look in anyone's face

Everybody has an opinion...

Folks are really good at telling you what they would do if they were you

The clear point of it was apparent: I'm not them and they

Surely aren't me

Good advice, yes, I will take into consideration

What I'm not about to take is someone telling me

What to do because they're a control freak

My son wasn't even on this earth for a full

Week and I was already bumping heads with Tim's mom

I was following the doctor's instructions for my son's

jaundice

Anything else was irrelevant, as well as the person it

came from

I didn't need anyone's home remedies or what they did

way back when

Prior to my son's birth I let everyone know what I would

And would not allow to be done to or around my child

I guess they thought I was playing

So, I guess I had to remind them

There are people in this world that know best about

everything

They always have an opinion about how

One should go about handling business

Even when they don't know what that business is…

Tim's mom was one of these people

She had something to say about everything I did

However I did anything, she always had a better way

She worked in healthcare and in her eyes that made her an expert

She knew better than the doctor's instructions

I needed to use different bottles

I should do this or that differently

If anything she said made sense

If they were suggestions and not commands

I would have taken some into consideration

But her delivery was not becoming

She would nag him to tell me things

Which didn't help anything

So now I had to put him in his place

Inform him to relay the same message to his mom

I did give the choice of him doing it or I could

He did not want the latter…

I'm sure she didn't like my request for her to back off

Just as I'm even more sure that I didn't care

And because of this I could see the rain clouds forming

It's partly sunny with a chance of showers

I couldn't wait to get home away from all the chatter

The doctor had given my son a clean bill of health

After that final local doctor's visit that morning

I was loading up the car

My family already knew that I was

Leaving as soon as I got the "OK" from the doctor

Tim's family... not so much

Again his mommy knew best

So again, heads were bumping

It was tiresome, to say the least

Even when I was pregnant she had told me what to eat

That I shouldn't eat hot sauce

I told her if I want hot and spicy, I am going to eat hot and spicy

I am a firm believer that the ignorant find ways try to overcompensate

With the little smarts they do have for the vast majority that they don't

I've heard that babies bring life to one's life or home

And that may be true in some cases

But this wasn't one of them

He was my son to raise not hers

He was here to give me purpose not fill her potential void

He's not here to be used as a bargaining tool of any sort

If you do for him, then do it because you love him

Don't do it just to have some type of leverage

To say "well I did this…" or "if it wasn't for me…"

Sadly, his mom was that type of person

Main reason why we needed to go back home

To get away from the nay-sayers

I was back in my element

I was in familiar territory now

That birthing stage was over

Now it was just taking care of this kid

I can do this part…

I'm used to this part

My son is in his own space

We are settling into our routine

I was holding firm on the things said by the older generation

Women like my Mamie, who birthed and raised a whole bunch of kids

Their words were my playbook

My grandmother was my go-to gal

This kid was mine

There was no sharing of duties

No rules coming from other people

It was all on me

Our routine was not all that hard to set up

You could have set your clock by this kid

This may be a little presumptuous... but

My son was perfect!

I was a proud mama already

Chapter Thirteen

A Light Drizzle, Part II

The days were passing by

My son was chill as usual

We were going about our day

Then my homegirl Keke called, my long-time friend

We talked as usual and then she said "Brace yourself"

Now what the beep was she saying this for?

Her tone was to calm me down and not create an uproar

Since she knows me so well she made sure

That I told her I would stay calm and not do anything

Her words: "I'm not telling you this to start anything, and don't let it cause problems in your house. I'm telling you so you will know who you are dealing with."

After that disclaimer, she told me the tale

She called Tim's parents house looking for me to no avail

But then his mother's called her phone back

She informed Keke that I was no longer there

Then she continued to speak about how I took Tim from her

How I didn't know what I'm doing because my son had thrush

There were several other things that were said

Things that came out the top of her head

The only reason I didn't jump in my car and ride

Out was because I told her I would not say anything

And no... she wasn't lying. She didn't have kids

So details like jaundice, or rashes, or thrush...

We never discussed

So, when she told me she called Tim's mom's house

Looking for me and his mom decided to

Talk about me I knew it was true

The things she said about my son...

Things I never told her

I had no choice but to accept its truth

This grown woman told my friend –

Someone she would consider a child –

What she thought I was doing wrong regarding my son

And how I took her son away

What in all the hells was this?!

Of course, I flipped, and my girl had to talk me off the

ledge

This was sheer stupidity that I couldn't deal with

Another friend of mine, Ann, that knew this family

before me

Had forewarned me about his mom

And now it was confirmed

I won't say anything to her or him

But I can assure you…

My silence will be deafening

Sometimes conversations can bring on troubles

I look for mine to be relaxing... healthy... even refreshing...

Not much of that was occurring with my conversations, regretfully

I moved past the stupidity of Tim's mother

For the sake of my son

For the sake of this family unit I was trying to create

I continued to do what was best for this kid

But the clouds didn't go away

Then came the light drizzle

Another phone call came

And with it the rain

It wasn't expected... this call

The information it delivered wasn't malicious

It was a form of ignorance that could take one's breath away

More stupidity

So now the question was...

Should I leave or stay?

It's said that if someone accuses you of something

Then that means they themselves are guilty of it

This friend, an old schoolmate, informed me that I was

A topic of conversation in a barbershop

My so-called "spouse" decided to lie about

My fidelity to his sibling

This sibling felt the need to repeat this nonsense

To folks who know nothing about me

Sadly, you never know who you're sitting next to

When you repeat things with no proof

Then how stupid does that make you

Now in the midst of my supposed infidelity I passed

By my so-called "spouse" in a car full of guys and waved

My friend wanted me to know what was being put out

In the universe about me

Even he knew that story was not to be believed

If I was being unfaithful why would I've allowed Tim to see me

I was standing in the rain, and Tim was defaming my name

While I was trying to create a family unit

He, on the other hand, was creating his escape

It's always best to be as real as possible

I put up with his frequent visits to his parents' home

I tried not to add unnecessary pressures

I didn't create extra bills

I wasn't spending money on things not needed

I was delaying my schooling because I didn't

Want to trouble him for money for fees

So, what was the need for this idiotic lie?

If he wanted out, he could have just said it

Don't create a problem to give oneself an excuse

I was unable to handle this particular lie

Mainly because I didn't understand why

I packed mine and my son's things and said goodbye

Unlike him, I was man enough to look him in his eyes

Some people need companionship

They have to be attached to someone

I guess it's nice to have a title of some sort

I assume coming home to a body is important

But recognizing that body as an actual

Person appears to be trying

When that body packs her things and leaves

Now he wants to be crying

I had no tears, just anger and frustration

Now he missed me... Now it was empty

He wanted me close just to make him feel something

All of this was for nothing

Trying to make good choices

Trying to grow up and not hold grudges

Trying not to be nasty because of past deeds

Look where all this trying had gotten me

I was back home, at my mother's house, mad

Trying to figure things out

This dude was calling constantly

And I was trying not to scream and shout

He wanted to work on us

That idiotic lie just proved that he wanted his space

But I wanted space too...

Out of my current situation

Out of this rain

Out of this insanity

Out of this pain

He got what he wanted

He was free to do whatever

This lie gave him his freedom

So why call me saying he'd been to the hospital

Blaming his diagnosis on me being gone?

Sweetie you had a nose bleed... carry on

It's true that we share a son, I thought,

So I have to see what's going on

I'm outside of myself in this moment

I don't know what or how

What am I doing right now?

How is what I'm doing going to make things alright?

I'm doing things I would have never done before

I guess I'm hurt or confused...

I sought out comfort through bottles of booze

This became a nightly thing

Hanging out and drinking

And going to clubs

My friend Keke was making me meet guys

Before I would say no, but I didn't this time

Keke was happily surprised

After I would put my son to bed, I headed

To the club instead of to sleep

What was the point of trying to create this family unit?

Who cares what I do and with whom?

I guess I wanted to know how it felt to be free

But this so-called freedom cost me

Cost me dearly

This person I was being wasn't thinking clearly

I wasn't keeping up with anything

I was being free…

I was chilling with this new guy

He seemed nice enough

It was something to do

Meanwhile my so-called "spouse" was popping up

Wanting to see our son

He had his mom believing his story that I had moved on

Moved on with whomever I was being unfaithful with

While we were still together

So, yes, words were exchanged between me and his mother

Because I'd had it

I was 'bout sick of these fools; Tim and his people

If I was so wrong or bad

Then why come into my presence at all?

I was spiraling head-first toward a dangerous fall

A fall into a place I had no business being in at all

In the midst of "me doing me"

I lost track of the one who came from me

After my now typical outing

After leaving my son in the bed asleep

Knowing that my mom was under the same roof

After becoming used to doing this very thing and

Everything being ok

After one of my usual outings one night… everything

would change

I walked in the room and my son was gone

I looked in the room my mom was sleeping in

I didn't see him there either

This buzz I had was now gone

It was replaced with panic

The place wasn't that big

So where could he go

I was so out of it, I was looking inside the washer and

behind doors

I was freaked all the way out now

Where is my son?

I went back in his room

Something led me to look

Down the side of the bed next to the wall

This is where I found my son

On the floor in the gap

I was sickened and devastated and mad at myself

This could have easily been the night my son took his

last breath

His head was inches away from a floorboard

With a nail in it

I grabbed him and held him close all night

I cried as if he did lose his life

But it was me who'd lost her life

I had lost my way

Because of my choices

I almost lost my baby

I need to get myself together

I am not in a good place

I am not ready to suffer the consequences I may

Have to face from being in this not so good space

I need to move on from here

Maybe I need to go back home with Tim

I am not good here on my own

But that reconciliation will be delayed

While I was having an out-of-body experience

And not paying attention to myself

I failed to realize I had missed a few steps

I was getting sick over the smell of certain foods

Feeling nauseous throughout the day

This was not normal for me

Then one day when Tim was visiting, he pointed out that the same

Always pad had been sitting in the same spot since I moved

Into my mom's house

He was right, but I never noticed

I just thought that all my drinking had messed things up...

So I went to get checked and it was confirmed

I was pregnant... AGAIN

This was not the plan

And now Tim was saying it wasn't his

It wasn't like I'd been gone long

It wasn't like we'd been separated for months

I couldn't understand how he could say that

Then again; I guess I could

The drizzle turned to rain

The rain created a flood

I already had a baby

What would I possibly do with another?

Since there was some doubt in the air... in his air

He decided to bring my mom into the mix

I was clear about things

I counted days out on my calendar

But for some reason he insisted on getting her involved

She didn't know nothing about nothing

I think he wanted to make me look bad

And I think she enjoyed the show

Now I was no longer perfect in her eyes

I really didn't care at this point

He had his moment and she had hers

After all was said and done

He and I had to figure out how we were going to carry on

My son was only 6 months old

I couldn't mentally handle dealing with two infants

I did it before with my siblings' kids

I wouldn't get any type of break with two

Money was already tight

He was already working day and night

We were barely keeping our heads above water

And this would drown us both

So, we talked it out...

I was going to have an abortion

The appointment was made and we went

It sounds crazy to say, but I was scared

I looked around that place with fear in my eyes

My ears were appalled by the conversations they heard

Women speaking on the number of abortions

they've had

Each abortion mentioned as casually as weather

I felt like I was in jail again, however brief

Somewhere I had no business being

I didn't want to be there, but I couldn't leave either

They gave me an ultrasound to confirm how far along I was

They stood where I couldn't see the monitor

And called out how many weeks I was

"You are 6 weeks and some days AND 7 weeks and some days"

My heart stopped and my eyes began to water

All I could say was "What?!"

I asked if I could look

Then I asked if I could have a moment

I went to tell Tim what I just heard

I then asked what he wanted to do

Then he asked me the same question too

I didn't want to bring two more into this world

With the uncertainty of knowing that they would be well taken care of

And I couldn't say with certainty that they would...

So, we chose to move forward

A piece of my soul was removed along with those embryos

I had no words when it was all over

I carried a blank stare on my face for days

I looked at my son with guilt in my eyes

Did he know what his mommy did?

Did he feel the emptiness inside of me now?

Did he know that they were there and now they are gone?

These were my thoughts as I glazed into his eyes

How will I ever explain this choice to my son?

All I know, right now, is that I have to move on

The phrase "it's easier said than done" proved to be true

I knew I had to move on from this loss

But I didn't know how, because I was lost

There were days when my smile wasn't a front

Then there were others where I couldn't even put one on

My homegirl Janell, who knew what I did, would call to check on me

She would ask "How are you doing?"

Some days I could answer that I was OK

Other days I didn't want to say

But I told her that I was doing ok anyway

I'm pretty sure she knew it was a lie

Then there were days when she asked that same question...

And all I could do was cry

I did the right thing, at least I hope I did

Lord, please forgive me!

There was no way I could care for three small kids

I know I will have to account for this one day

And I'm ok with it

But Lord please make sure it comes back on me

I don't want my son to pay for the things I've done

So, for my son I have to do better

Chapter Fourteen

The Unseen, Part I

Loss has its way of pulling people together

It can make you stay when you want to go

It can make you go back

Even when you can't look at them no more

This loss created a ripple effect that I couldn't see at first

I went back to try and work things out

I don't know if this was for my sake

Or my baby's

Tim and I had shared a loss

Of something I couldn't find again

I couldn't fix it, couldn't make things better

I just knew that I was standing smack dead in the

Middle of bad weather

I don't know how our interaction will be

I don't know if he will use this against me

I don't know where we go from here

I'm in uncharted territory

I have no way of seeing what's in store for me

Right now, the future is unclear

And I can't do anything but stand in this spot

We were trying to get back to some type of normalcy

We moved into a different place

That had a little more space

Closer to the school that I would be starting at soon

We worked my class schedule around his at work

I was finally about to do what I moved away to do

We got engaged...

I said "yes" because it was a part of my life plan

To be married with kids and a career

Which may not have been happening in order

But it was happening

Something is better than nothing, I guess

I was determined to create

And maintain this family unit

Or something close to it

I started school and I was excited

I didn't need to pay any fees

I was a transfer student so fees were waived

Which meant I didn't have to ask Tim for any money

I know it's sad to feel that way

I know one should be able to depend on a spouse

Or so they say

I was just not in that season

I took issue with giving a person the opportunity

To say "if it wasn't for me…"

Him using that statement I could definitely see

So, yes, I was happy I was able to avoid that possibility

I was happy that I was doing something for me

Would the family benefit from this, eventually?

Yes…

But mainly it was for me

School has always been for me

In many ways my earthly escape

The only place where I owned my space

My mistakes, my choices, my existence in this

Area was totally dependent upon me

If I screwed up, it was all on me

Whatever went on in this period I controlled

This may seem overwhelming for some

But for me it was welcoming

I was looking forward to the challenge

It provided balance

I was going to class, coming home to my baby

And contributing some funds to the household

I felt useful again…

I should have been tired and grumpy

But I was not

I had a purpose other than just being a mother

(And yes, being a mother is all well and fine

But that's not all I wanted to be)

I had obligations as a student now

Yes, it was difficult at times

Life does happen

And it happens more unexpectedly with a kid

But I managed…

Although there was another adult in the home

I still carried on as if I was alone

I went to class in the mornings

While Tim went to work in the evenings

This would alleviate the need for daycare

Which would have created another bill

I couldn't contribute monetarily

However, I could minimize our expenses

My son was asleep while I went to class

So, there wasn't much for this person to do

Until there was...

Until this infant became mobile

Until you have to pay attention to the 9-month-old

Even in your sleep

Until common sense tells you to close the bedroom

Door back after you open it from going to take a piss

Until I walked through the door

After coming back from class and saw my son

Falling down the steps

It felt like it only took me two steps to get to him

To comfort him and reassure him that

Everything was ok

To wonder had this happened any other time

Before today

I was now full of rage

It was about to be all kinds of hell to pay

How can anyone allow this to happen to their baby?

The sad part is that Tim didn't even wake up

After hearing all this

That made it even worse

My son could get into whatever and this clown

Would not hear a thing

Maybe it's just a mother's instinct

(That kid couldn't twitch too often without

Me waking up)

With all these thoughts racing through my mind

I jumped up with fire in my eyes

I went off on him and the blank look on his face

To hell and back I went

Absolutely nothing could explain away

What just happened

All I knew was he had better be happy nothing

Was fractured

Needless to say, things went downhill after that day

It's not like all was going great anyway

There weren't many pleasant talks between us two

But we managed and that was cool

But now my words with Tim are short and precise

I'm not foreseeing a near future of people

Throwing rice

Indeed, I know that people do make mistakes

What gets me is when they don't own up to them

My baby was fine, and no real harm was done

I just couldn't deal with this dude and

His short-lived maturity runs

My love for Tim had long gone away

I only stayed because we'd procreated

He was now returning to our hometown often

He was constantly hanging out with the female

Neighbor next door

And my ignorance wouldn't allow me to think

That something was going on

His activities didn't concern me

I wasn't looking for any indiscretions on his part

He worked and hung out

I went to school and stayed home

I had my baby, so it's not like I was alone

This went on for some time

Until the night he crossed the line

I woke up after falling asleep with my son and Tim was gone

His car was still there and so was his phone

He was not at the neighbor's; it didn't sound like

Anyone was home

There was no note in sight

So where could this dude be in the middle

Of the night?

I now decided to go through his phone

And now I saw why this dude wasn't home

I saw a lot of back and forth between him

And some chick

A whole lot of "baby" and "sweetie" being shared

What in the hell was this shit?

I was now seeing red

All I wanted was for this dude to be dead

I was back and forth looking out the window

Because I wanted to see

I wanted to see the chick that was calling him baby

I now had a knife in my hand

This dude assumed I was playing

I called my girl Janell, so she wouldn't be shocked when

She saw me on TV for murdering this creep

She was trying to calm me down

But she didn't see

This was all about principles to me

Until she said "What about your baby? What's

going to happen to him if you do this?"

And she was right...

I knew what would happen to me

I couldn't leave him in this world without Mommy

All people do is lie

Then when they get caught in those

Lies they wanna cry

Or point the finger and place blame

Whatever it is that you do

Own it… don't be ashamed

He was doing nothing but spewing a bunch of lies

Lies that clearly went against what

I saw with my own eyes

He said he went next door

But I saw him coming through a cut in the

Trees that led to the street

He said the chick from his phone was just a friend

He was trying to make it seem like it was all me

Like I didn't see none of what I'd just seen

He said I could call her and she would

Tell me the same thing

So, I agreed and went to sleep

I would call her and we would see

I'm not big on nagging folks

So, I went about my regular routine

I made no mention of what occurred that night

Couldn't do anything but move on

No need to continue to fuss and fight

After all I was doing what was best for my baby... Right?

So, I thought, let's move on...

Let's continue to be this family unit that's not

A real family

Just people residing under the same roof

If there was any real love in this place

I couldn't see any proof

So, yes, physically I was there

But mentally I was getting myself prepared

Emotionally I honestly didn't care anymore

Never again would I wonder what was going

On when he exited that door

I was nobody's fool

I was just waiting for the semester to end

And when the semester ended this would too

Until then me and my son would be sleeping

In the other room

We started to spend separate times with our son

There wasn't much room to be together

In this weather

When bedtime came

Play time was over

I didn't really care if he was just getting home

From "working over" at the job

Petty would show up every now and again with Tim

He would intentionally do childish things once

We began to sleep in the other room

Because I didn't want to deal with petty

I began locking the door before we went to sleep

I wanted my baby to be comfortable

And I wanted to sleep in peace

Little did I know…

And never would have I expected…

A night came where I woke up with Tim

On top of me naked

I was stunned

I was confused

I was worried, to say the least

What did this guy just do?

Why is he… How did he undress me?

Did he just do what I think he did

With our baby lying next to me?

Why would he do this?

What was he thinking?

And when I asked…

He chuckled and told me he could do whatever

He wanted to me

I guess, in his mind, this was true because we were a couple

And because of this he had rights to me

I can't begin to try to understand or explain

What he meant

The only thing I did know was….

This was it!

I did not feel safe around this guy anymore

He could try and pick the lock again

But I would now lock and barricade this bedroom door

It felt like time was moving slowly

I was ready to go because this guy was acting funny

If we did ride in the same vehicle

I rode in the back with my son

Tim was talking to our pastor and

Trying to get us to go to counseling

But the thing about counseling is…

If you're not honest about it all

Then none of it works

And here again it was all on me

Just because I'm straight up and to the point

Then it was: see, look, she's so mean

Whomever can call it whatever they want

I'm just being me

So, whomever can like it, love it, or leave

If it ain't one damn thing, it's another

My Honda Prelude went down and now I have to buy a new car

I went through a friend of a friend

They'd been around for some time, so I was

Sure that I was in good hands

They found me a car and things seemed to be ok

I was heading back home and it started acting crazy

I had just gotten on the highway, hadn't got too far

My mom and brother came to drive the car

Back to my mother's house

It'd only been sitting at her house for a few weeks

And from there my car was stolen

I didn't know why this storm was holding

The friend helped me through the process of this

Nightmare, since I had no clue what to do

I met my friend's friend at my mom's house

To get some things together

To finalize replacing the car that was stolen

I don't know what happened or why it happened

I just know I ended up tussling with this guy for over an hour

He wanted sex and I didn't

He was here to help me, that was it

Regardless of if I liked who I was with or not

I surely wasn't going to cheat

I gave up after this hour or more

He got what he wanted on my old bedroom floor

I don't know what's wrong with me or why this

Keeps happening

This wasn't the first or second time a guy had

Forced themselves on me

In the midst of the tussle, my phone recorded

The whole ordeal

Obviously buttons were being pressed amid our tussle

I thought it made a call

But it just recorded it all

He seemed oblivious to what just occurred

I guess the words "no" or "stop" were never heard

I called Janell to ask her what I should do

I went to her and let her listen to what

Had happened in that room

I refused to be a victim

I didn't want my other friend to see what her

Friend had done to me

Was this another "wrong place, wrong time"

That I'd gotten myself into

I'm at a loss

This was something I would never have foreseen

I don't think I'm awake

I hope this is all a bad dream

So, what had occurred was real

But I had no idea how to feel

Was it just me??

Had there been clues that I'd been missing?

I was trying to figure out what was going on with me

Meanwhile this guy was calling me all happy

He was really acting like this was something

That was supposed to have happened

I was avoiding the topic at all costs

Could it be that this guy was far gone?

Did he truly feel that I was putting on?

I was unsure of my next step

So I focused on how to not let this affect me

And the first thing on that list was

Finding something to kill this sperm inside of me

So, I switched my focus from the before to the after

...I wasn't raped...

I was just stupid and careless

This was what I told myself

This was what happened

This was me rewriting the entire script

Of this poorly written chapter

I was now in control of the

Before... during... and after

There was another saying that I'd

Heard throughout the years

It was along the lines of

"If you go looking for it, you will find it"

The semester was nearing its end

Which meant I was still living with my

Soon to be ex

For reasons unknown to me

Tim was going through my things

I found that he had gone through my

Papers from school

He was looking through my car

To which he had, at some point

Gone and made a key

He had gone through my jacket pockets

Where he found a vaginal contraceptive film

Something that shouldn't have belonged to me

This created quite the dilemma

A dilemma that made me look sketchy

(People fail to see their own mess

Even though they can clearly see all of yours)

He now owed his workplace money

He worked in two different departments

That required separate clocks to be punched

But he decided to ride them both

And now he owed money for stealing time

He just lied to my face

He didn't go to meet with Janell's husband about a job

I was literally on the phone with her when

He lied through his teeth

And let's not forget about the fact that

He was a cheat

But none of that mattered when

He thought he had found proof against me

He could now say he had proof that I'd been cheating

I honestly considered letting him think whatever

He wanted to think

But his entire aura about what he thought

He'd found just wouldn't let me be

So, I told him the truth about why

He found the VCF

Of course, he didn't believe me

That would mean he could no longer feel

Justified for what he'd done or was doing

I had more than just my words

I had Janell, who knew the truth

I don't know if he actually believed her or not

All I did know was all his idiotic

Accusations had to stop

But since this was who he wanted me to be

I would give him something to see

Chapter Fifteen

The Unseen, Part II

I went about things in a very screwed-up way

My methods may cause confusion

Disgust and even anger in others

But it made sense to me

Or at least it helped me move past things

I guess my way of processing the devastation

May not have been all that great or healthy

But this way… I wasn't a victim

I preferred to feel a person's anger

Than deal with their pity toward my circumstances

I never wanted nor will I ever need someone to feel

sorry for me

Honestly… what would that do to help me?

Therefore, I made a choice

Probably selfish and self-centered

But I felt it was necessary

Considering the fact that I was leaving Tim

I was moving back home

I was going to be living with my mom

I was starting over with a kid in tow

There was just too much too soon

I felt like I'd been constantly walking into a dark room

So, yes, I decided to give this guy, Will, a chance

I knew that he would provide for me

And since he'd already gotten the

Very thing I was trying to keep

I may as well give it to him freely

And in exchange he can take care of me and my baby

The semester had come to an end

I parted ways with Tim

And even though he was out there messing

Around with who knows what

He still seemed shocked and upset about us breaking up

I didn't think he could act or be

Any dumber than what I'd previously seen

Clearly that was wrong of me

Of course, the situation that occurred with me was now all a lie

No one forced themselves on me, I was just covering up my cheating

That was the reason why I was leaving

That's why I was saying goodbye

It wasn't because he, himself, had cheated on me

In Tim's altered universe I was leaving him to be with

the other guy

None of his actions over the last five years had nothing

To do with anything

I had no desire to argue or fuss

I just knew things were over between us

Boys can be so silly sometimes

When things don't go their way

They have a meltdown

Tim was doing stupid things

He began stalking me

He was coming to my mom's house just to start

arguments with me

He even tried to fight me for the apartment key from

our old place

I still had belongings there that I had to move

He got what little things he owned

Which was his clothes and nothing more

Well... he did pay for a mattress set for our baby

Which he took

Meaning it didn't make sense for him to

Be trying to get my key

As it stood right now

This dude was being pretty petty

I couldn't understand why he was carrying on this way

In his eyes, I was cruel for not understanding his feelings

All I did know was

There was not too much more I could take

But the pettiness continued...

I thought that things would take their course

He would get over it and move on

My thoughts were all wrong

Not sure when or how

But it appeared that my mom was on his side

Clearly I, her mean daughter, wronged Tim somehow

And yet, he keyed my car...

He had a female who had kids with his cousin call me

Asking me why I was talking about her

Needless to say, I went off on her

I didn't even know her

But she was the one who decided to ring my phone

The list of trifling occurrences just continued to grow

Though my mother acted as if he could do no wrong

I was somehow the culprit

I was the villain in all this

I was there trying to take care of my child

Meanwhile his "donor", Tim, was running wild

He admitted to me that his so-called friend

May be pregnant with his baby

I'm human, so yes, I did shed a tear

That was something my ears did not need to hear

Throughout the years he was trying to paint me as the villain

Clearly, he moved on way before me

Now there was a current chick that he was comparing to me

And still, none of this my mother noticed or acknowledged

Because I'm so nasty and mean

Titles that I did not earn nor deserved

I didn't know how to treat Tim

I took advantage of him because he is so sweet

I probably scared him because I'm so mean

So, I guess I deserved all that was happening to me

It's hard to let go of a long-held dream

I was supposed to have a healthy family unit

And now that dream was gone

In some ways I felt like a failure

That dream was swept under the table

I didn't know how much I was affected by this

Until a song played on the radio station's playlist

I released uncontrollable tears

And with these tears came all of my fears

I was now somebody's "baby mama"

Must take that title and deal with the drama

Everyone else decided to create

I'm standing and looking at this journey...

I do not want to walk through those gates

My dad was still in jail

And even though I was around family

I felt like I was in hell... ALONE

I had my two homegirls Janell and Keke, and my little

brother

From another mother, and Mamie, and I had

My oldest sibling to some extent

But she had her own break-up going on

There was only so much any of them could do

They provided moral support

And in that moment, it had to be enough

I was utterly confused at how my mom

Could turn her back on one she gave birth to

In all my trouble I moved in with my mom simply

because

I didn't have anywhere else to stay

I foolishly thought, if bad went to worse, that she would

turn to me

The devastation of her constant betrayal will never go

away

Tim was her kid now

She didn't even see me

Or what she did see wasn't me

She saw whatever version she created of me

And I'm pretty sure that version had my father standing next to me

So how was I to handle this?

I was fighting with my ex, my mom,

And now my second oldest sibling

I felt trapped in this mess

There was nothing I could do

There was no one for me to address

Common sense or logic eluded my mother's presence

No matter what I said to her

She acted as if I hadn't said anything at all

I don't understand how a parent can enjoy

Seeing their own fall

And yes, I was falling

I'd been falling for a while

It just didn't look that way

After all, I was standing on what appeared to be solid ground

But the ground I was on was hot to the touch and deafening to the ears

A ground that immobilized me

Because it covered every last one of my fears

I was spiraling out of control

And those closest to me didn't even really know

How close I'd come to permanently closing my doors

The thoughts visited me from time to time

But how could I... Me and my son's life is forever intertwined

I don't want to do this anymore

I reached out to the pastor from my old church

I was looking for guidance

I wanted someone's help

Although she spoke encouraging words

There was just too much that she didn't know

Therefore, she couldn't give me words for exactly

What I was needing

I've tried to kneel, Lord

But it's not helping with the healing

I know that should have been the way to go

But it wasn't helping me to understand those feelings

Of hurt, anger, loneliness, betrayal, and failure

I need my daddy...

I need my Superman...

I thought: I wouldn't be going through this

If he was here to help me stand

I know you may say that he's just a dad

But my dad was no ordinary man

I got a call one day... from my one and only dad

He was scheduled to come home soon and I was oh so glad

He asked how I was doing

I told him what was going on

He told me to read the book of Job

He said that after I read that

I would see that I didn't really have that much going on

If anyone else had made that statement

I would have probably taken offense

But since it was him, it made so much sense

I then outlined my issues with my mom

I asked him why she was treating me this way

He then said "I'm sorry to tell you, sweetie, but she doesn't like you. You have more of me in you than any of the others. So, things will always be different for you"

He went a little more in depth

But his explanation didn't minimize the tears I shed

I was at a loss for words

How could my own mother not like me?

Was this since birth, or did her distaste for me grow gradually?

I guess it did explain her treatment of me

So now I had to suck it up and move on

I was going to do what my dad said

I was going to read the book of Job

Hopefully that reading would help me navigate the road

Even though things were hectic

I didn't want this foolishness to affect my baby

Yes, Tim was being super stupid

But that was with me

I didn't want to use any of his actions as reason

For him not to see the baby

So I allowed him to come and get his child

I was not hindering his efforts to be a dad

I was still trying to go to school

He wasn't working, so he could have watched our kid during this time

(If one doesn't have the money to spend

One could at least spend the time)

But he didn't see it this way

He wanted to get him sporadically

When I needed him to keep my son, he was nowhere to be found

When I asked when was he going to see him

He told me that he didn't have time

It appeared as if he couldn't see or deal with me

He didn't want to deal with nor see his seed

Adult problems shouldn't become a problem for a kid

My son had nothing to do with this

He didn't ask to be here

He didn't ask to be a part of this situation

There is something wrong when you isolate

Yourself from your own kid due to a failed relationship

Time is supposed to heal all wounds

But when they are self-inflicted, then just deal with it, dude

Months had passed and we both should have grown

He was stuck on the fact that I was no longer his pawn

No longer would I beg him to see his child

It was proving to be a waste of time

Therefore, I was done with it

The days went by and I allowed myself

To begin to spend time with Will

Regardless of how things started

I allowed myself to pursue things... just guarded

Will helped me get another car, again

After the break-in and vandalism at the hands of Tim

He felt uneasy and didn't want to wait for what could come next

He could clearly see that Tim was deranged

All the back and forth with him was insane

He didn't want to see my son

But then again he would if there could be a we

I hate you I love you became his thing

So, securing another vehicle for me

Was Will's way of making sure me and my baby were safe

And that small gesture created even more chaos

Constant chatter began to follow me

I would catch them rolling their eyes at me

My mom, the second born, and members of my mom's family

Felt the need to show me how much they disliked what I was doing

Although I wasn't doing anything but trying to live a life

Not even my life, just some form of a life

Not sure why people weren't happy for me

My business was my business

I wasn't that close with my family

The gossip and judgement of people was real

All anyone saw was what was presented to them by me

I surely wasn't going to share, with family, my vulnerability

After all, that caring meter didn't shift too far from empty

So it didn't matter what my ex did

All eyes were on me

It was inconceivable to the family that this new guy would secure

Transportation for me and my kid

Even though none of this would have been

Necessary if my ex didn't decide to cheat on me

Blame me for his shortcomings and accuse me of

cheating

I wouldn't have had to do what I had done... leave

If this guy would have just grown up

And been a father to his son

It appears like everything now is about Will

Tim and my mom were in cahoots

Clearly I wasn't thinking for myself

Will had taken control of me and who knows what else

If a damn bird fell out of the sky

Will was the reason why

I wasn't trying to please anyone

I just wanted to take care of my son

And in the midst of trying to do what I needed to do

A year or more had passed

I wound up pregnant again

Pregnant by the new dude

Will had been around for some time now

My son had become familiar with him

He didn't really have much of a choice

Since the real dad didn't want to be around his own child

Trust that I'm not making that statement lightly

It was a hard fact that I no longer wanted to fight

Tim would randomly pop-up to my mother's house

No intentions on picking up his kid

It was done because he knew he could get away with it

My mother would let him inside at any time

Hating me but still wanting to look up in my face

He could move forward

But I was expected to march in place

One night he popped up and I was "well done"

This guy didn't even take a second glance at my son

He came only to attempt to berate me

However, when I mentioned how he wasn't spending

Time with his own son

Somehow his feelings got hurt

Now he wants to get confrontational

My oldest sister heard the commotion and told him to leave

The last words Tim said to me were

"I will do for that kid when it's convenient for me!"

These were his words during one of his fits

Then he said I needed to tell the other

Guy to take care of his kid

His words were precise and serious

So that's exactly what I did

The message was passed on to Will who eagerly accepted

Not sure why Tim felt the task would be rejected

So yes, he and my son were forming a bond

A bond that my son only previously had with his mom

I was starting to accept my recent physical condition

This was not something that I wanted or planned

I didn't want to have another kid by a different man

But it's something that I was willing to deal with

Yes, I was taking precautions

But his offense outplayed my defense

So now, again, I had to adjust my plans for another kid…

And I did

There was definitely no room for any foolishness

Which meant, the absence of the ex was not missed

My son was healthy and happy

And that's all that mattered to me

He was getting some form of male attention

And while I was giving him everything I had

That was something that he couldn't get from me

As I began to show

It caused the unnecessary drama to show up even more

I was greeted with various obstacles

There were issues with my pregnancy

My mom would glance at me evilly

I soon figured out what it all meant

When my ex came for my son

With no warning or phone call

Might I remind you…

He hadn't been around at all

So, I'm not sure why he thought he could come and

Take my son from me

I told him to go…

We could make arrangements for another day

But today my son couldn't go with him

He tried to throw my kid in the car to the girlfriend

Tim instructed her to lock the door

But I was able to get a hand in

I took my son from her

And Tim came at me again

We were now in the street tussling...

I was looking around to see if someone was coming to my aid

Then I saw my sister, the second born, coming from behind me

As I was about to release a sigh of relief

I quickly realized she wasn't there for me

She was helping this guy take my kid

To this day she shows no regret for what she did

And as if that wasn't enough

My mom declared, later, that she would have done the same thing

She also would have helped Tim kidnap my kid

Pregnant and all

I was ready to brawl

But I know that I couldn't

So, I called the police so I could get my kid

I couldn't believe what just happened

I couldn't believe what my so-called family just did

This entire situation could have gone...

No, should have gone a totally different way

I shouldn't have been in the street, pregnant, fighting

off my ex

And my sister for the sake of my baby

Before the sun set

I got my son back

And almost lost the other all in the same day

I began to cramp with horrific pains

After all of the commotion

I was hospitalized due to having heavy bleeding

Stayed for a few days for me and my unborn to do some

healing

Chapter Sixteen

The Unseen, Part III:

I Forgot to Mention...

After I left, when Tim decided to spread that lie

Having his family believe that I was riding around town

With a group of guys

The lease ran out on our old apartment

Therefore, he had moved to a townhome

This is where the unnecessary drama began to brew

Here is when he went to the hospital for an

Uncontrollable nosebleed

He called me and his mother

But it appeared as if I was the only one concerned

Yes, I went to go check on the father of my son

When I got there, he seemed fine to me

No blood nowhere...

Not on any tissue or even his shirt

No discharge papers were seen or shown

He didn't even cough up a diagnosis code

All he could do was express how I was

To blame for all of this

I was at fault for his current medical condition

He was stressed and missed me and his kid

I guess that was supposed to have proven something to me

He loved and missed us so much that it

Was shown through a nosebleed

I am not him...

And he is surely not me...

I can't rationalize his rationale about his feelings for me

It was confusing at best

A little stupid to say the least

He was ok and I was ready to leave

While I was trying to finish up this discussion

This guy pulls out a ring and proposes to me

This is something I didn't see coming

I accepted his proposal reluctantly

Even told him I would take but not wear the ring

That was not an option he was prepared to greet

So, I agreed to wear his ring

It was supposed to be a joyous occasion

And yet, none of this was joyful for me

I was going with my timeline of my life's plan

Didn't really matter that I wasn't in love with this man

So, after dealing with the grave situation, the abortion, that arose

While I was back home living with my mom

I moved back with him

Hoping that we could carry on

We were going to get married and become a solid family unit

We had just gone through the loss of two

So why shouldn't we do this

If not for me or him

Why not for them

Maybe they would come back after we made this right

After we were better prepared to offer

Them the best kind of care

So, we were going to start a registry

We were going to price and compare venues for our wedding

It wasn't a celebration

I didn't make an announcement or anything

If people saw the ring and asked if I was engaged

I'd agree with their findings

Couldn't care less if they were happy for me

I was talking dresses with one of my friends

Only because she was beginning to plan

Her own wedding

Sadly, I was more excited for her than myself

On the outside looking in... I needed some serious help

One would think that a marriage proposal

Would make a man tighten his belt

That wasn't the case here

This negro needed some help

Remember I mentioned waking up out of my sleep

And seeing this guy cutting through the trees

Coming from the street

Him claiming he was next door at the neighbor's

But he came from a different direction

Me ready to kill him

And my homegirl reminding me of this baby

That needed my love and affection

After him saying this chick in his phone

Was just a friend

Him inviting me to call her…

Well, a few days passed and that's exactly what I did

I called and questioned this so-called friend

How long have you known this guy?

Do you have pet names for all of your male friends?

She commenced to explain herself

She stated that they were indeed friends

The "boo," "baby," and "sweetie" was just how she spoke

She called everyone that

I asked, "Should I be offended that you've not

Said any of those to me?!"

She sounded confused

So, I recited what she'd just said to me

"If this is the manner in which you speak; then why haven't you

spoken those very words to me?"

She didn't really have a response

So that answered all of my questions

And I informed her that neither she nor he was slick

And that she could have him

And that I wasn't the average chick

I let her know that I called because he invited me to

And that I wanted – needed – to know if he was lying to me

But I did warn Tim that if I found out that she'd

Been around my kid

That she would see me

And I was a person she never wanted to meet

This was when I no longer cared

I was going through the motions

I was just living there

If whoever thought he was a catch

Let them keep him then

I was not about to chase behind or fight over no damn man

And this was when I gave the ring back

You don't propose to a person and continue

To do the same thing

If you have no desire to change

Then why present a ring like it's worth something

Yeah, things have been insane

But what you ain't gone do is handle me and my baby

Since his actions showed that he wanted his space...

I gave it to him

My son and I began to sleep in the other room

If he wanted to touch on her, that was fine by me

What he wasn't gone do is leave her and

Come home trying to touch on me

I didn't understand why this would have created

A problem; the distance was necessary

But for whatever insane reason

He just couldn't let it be

I guess that's why he decided to rape me

Yet in his eyes he did nothing to me

"We're together, I can do what I want, when

I want. You can't stop me"

All the while he said this with a smile

Since I'd been through this before

Back during my high school years

There were no emotions for me to explore

I already knew what they were

I just started putting a chair behind the door

It's obvious he got in by picking the lock

Which is why I decided to add a prop

This is when I made my final decision to leave

And with that I needed to prepare and plan

I'd heard of too many things that happen

When a woman tries to leave a man

My Prelude needed some regular maintenance

I had money for parts, but no money for labor

So, I asked my big brother for a favor

He didn't even pretend like he was going to help

I needed it done so I talked Tim through

The process of what needed to be repaired

It was actually simple enough to fix

Screw one thing out and another one in

Like a light bulb

But that task proved to be challenging

It worked briefly until it left me and my son stranded

It was my fault…

I shouldn't have asked him to try and rectify the

problem

He wasn't mechanically inclined

So, I got with one of my homegirls, Tee, who

Knew someone who could help

Tee got her mechanic to come and look at my car

We were able to get it to my mom's place

And from there I was told that I needed another car

There were a couple of things that could be tried with my car

But it wouldn't get very far

They had a vehicle that I bought

But as I mentioned, something went

Haywire with that car shortly after I got it

And this is where events happened that made

Things very bizarre

Trying to get everything worked out about

My new Civic being stolen

This was where I ended up on the floor tussling

For over an hour

This was where I was in the situation where it appeared

That I had no power

Again... this keeps happening

But I didn't involve the police

Because the tussle wasn't with a friend of a friend

It was actually my friend Tee's brother…. Will

We were close and I couldn't hurt her

I confided this to my homegirl, Janell

Tee and I were friends for a long time

The years were many and our friendship went deep

That's why I held it in

This is why I just let it be

I couldn't do that to her

And I didn't want to deal with the police

By this time, I had come across too many cops

That just don't believe what you say

I didn't want to be seen as an instigator or victim

So, to avoid all of that

I decided that it didn't really happen

When a female goes for a physical

There are standard questions and tests that are

performed

I had a physical at school

Nothing special or troubling… standard procedure

I didn't know I had to lock things away

At the time my "live-in", Will, was asking me

Random questions about the female

Anatomy and signs and symptoms of STDs

I was just answering them

There were no concerning thoughts in my

Mind about this line of questioning

It was funny to me

Until one day I couldn't find my car keys

I had looked everywhere two times over and

Was starting on round three

Until I called my live-in and asked if he'd seen my car

keys

It was a simple question

I was using a normal tone

But then his reaction was OFF in many ways

He had trouble answering

Which was very peculiar to me

There was no simple "yes" or "no"

Or "have you looked here" or "there"

His response was like he was intentionally

Trying to hide something

What that was exactly was unknown to me

I will admit that his behavior flipped a switch

So now I'm no longer asking

I'm demanding a straight-up answer concerning my keys

Through all of his noise I didn't get an answer

Until I threatened to call the pastor

Only then did he reveal that he had my keys

Why?

I demanded he bring me back my damn keys

Now this was about that time he was to meet

With Janell's husband about a job

So, he was complaining about how he was going to be late

As I looked in through the window of my car and

Saw things in places they had no business being

Only then did it come to me

He'd gone through my car and came across

A physical form from school

A wellness check from student health

A form that should be put away, because it is private

Was now only partially hidden under my passenger seat

I now see why he had all those questions about STDs

Me and Janell were in awe of the events that were

unraveling

All of this during his supposed traveling

While I was still on the phone with Janell

The live-in walked in

He told me that the guy called and rescheduled

Then he gave me my keys

Looking around as if to catch me or something

But I knew he had just told me a bold-faced lie

Janell's husband was asking her to ask me where he was

And I told her that he just walked through my front door

I had absolutely no words to say

Janell and I were both baffled by what had happened this day

Time was up, the semester was coming to an end

It would be time for me to leave

I couldn't put up with this

I was tired of all this crap happening to me

I forgot to mention that

All this chaos that surrounded me may have

Been due to the fact that this other guy, Will, was

Involved with someone and had kids

Tim was damning me to hell because I was involved with him

But for as far back as I could remember

I'd always seen Will with other women

He is Tee's older brother so he has always been in the picture

But that shouldn't minimize how my ex

Was treating me

I never spoke on any of the issues my ex and I had

Did that mean he was all good

And I was all bad?

Yes, the current guy's situation created an entire cluster-fuck

But still, certain people in my family allowed Tim to run amok

My choice made it easier for them to believe whatever

Deranged stories he had told to them

And not even them... told my mom

Either way; dislike what I do

Don't help some guy take down your kin

Don't let him see you leave me out here stranded

I didn't say how Tim was following me

How he had, publicly, put his hands on me

No one knew how he confessed to me

That another may be carrying his kid

But after I left him

She decided it wasn't his

Since I decided not to share this

I was an easy target to go against

Again, dislike what I do

Don't stand with another against me

Then expect me to respect you

Everything was all over the place

Regardless of the situation I was trying to be cordial

I don't have to like you to deal with you

Nothing is about me, it's about my son

So, if you helped make him

You need to help take care of him

Since Tim and his people didn't want to keep him

Then he could pay for someone who will

But he couldn't even do that, or didn't want to

Which left me with another bill

While at daycare my baby got sick

It required a few days stay in the hospital

And even here… there came some shit

My son had some type of virus that

Caused him not to hold in much he ate

My baby was miserable…

Tim came to the hospital

Pointing fingers of course

Then my mom came doing the same

She went as far as to speak with the nurse and defame my name

She caused this hospital official to

'Come at me sideways'

This nurse asked, "What are you feeding him; dirt?

Your mother said you don't feed him much."

Who knows what else was said

But she made it seem like whatever I fed him he

Should be dead...

Immediately I asked my mom what she had said

Her response was sheer stupidity that came

Off the top of her head

I was floored by the things she had just relayed to me

I'm not properly feeding my kid because I don't give

Him pork and beans

Yes, it was a staple food in my upbringing

And I'd had enough of it which is why I didn't feed it to my baby

I did the only thing I knew to do

I called my daddy!

My dad was home from jail

I was no longer in this fight alone

Yes, I got that there was only so much he could do

But it means everything when you know you have

Someone standing next to you

Chapter Seventeen

The In-Between

Life isn't all that it's cracked up to be

No matter what I tried to do

It seemed as if 'the bad' was always holding on to me

Every time I felt some type of relief

A hard, swift slap in the face by reality would remind me

And this reality was hard to release

Regardless of how hard I tried to change my thoughts

for the better

I some how awaited the bad weather

My mom was in cahoots with the enemy

Why else would she say the things she'd been saying

about me?

My dad did clear things up with the hospital staff

But he shouldn't have had to speak up for me

Against my own mother

My dad wasn't the only one to come to my defense

After telling Will what had happened

He was as angry as me

And with no disrespect he asked if he

And my mother could meet

And that meeting was so he could defend me

He'd seen how I was with my kid

So, for her to utter the words that she did

Made him livid

I will admit that it was refreshing to see

The looks on their faces as he was defending me

It was a shift to have a guy take up for me

Instead of talking about me

He was protective of me

And right now…

That was exactly what I needed

After giving birth to my second kid

I thought things would change

He took his first breath earlier than expected

It was known that this was going to happen

Again, I had issues throughout the pregnancy

Not to mention all the chaos that continued to stress me

So, me and my baby held on for as long as we could

Longer than expected

And long enough for the medication I was given to

Do what it should

I wasn't worried about giving birth early

While pregnant, now and before,

I prayed that they would be healthy and happy when they

Entered this world

And that's exactly what he was

My oldest, Duncan, came to see the new kid

He was mad at me...

He said that I left him to go and have a baby

Not even three years of age yet

My boy was always expressive about his feelings with me

So, we had a discussion

And all was well until the new baby, Liam, started fussing

He was ok with his new little brother coming Home with me

This was going to be quite an adjustment

We were both so used to it being 'him and me'

And now we were going to be three

I can deal with this... I hoped

But Liam came in swinging

Like Tarzan on a rope

It didn't seem hard to adjust with Duncan

Things seemed pretty simple to me

But this new one proved to be a bit more challenging

He made absolutely nothing simple for me

Feeding him was a task

He couldn't keep down anything he ate

There were constant visits to the doctor

This became a frequent date

Liam ended up on several meds just so he could eat

This kid was constantly keeping me on my feet

He cried constantly

And I was not totally sure why

When he was not so needy, he was great

But when the floodgates opened, this I hated

Liam would disrupt Duncan when he would try and sleep

His cry was so loud

It made us both uneasy

This kid was new, cute, and cuddly

People like to play with infants…

Which was a much-needed distraction

Since it reduced some tension between my mother and I

So, for that I was thankful for my mother

She would get him if only for that fact

And I was eternally grateful

Because the little one was going to get smacked

I was overwhelmed

I was frustrated

His dad would come to visit

But I berated the guy

Don't come just to check on him and say 'Hi'

I needed for him to take his kid

Me and Duncan needed a break

Liam wouldn't stop…

He wouldn't let me breathe, for God's sake

I'm not afraid to admit when I'm wrong

He made me sick!!

And I was wrong for feeling the way that I did towards a newborn

After all, he was my kid

I didn't want to hurt him

Although, sometimes, I felt like I did

I was just frustrated when he wouldn't respond

To anything that I did

I'd play with him, feed him, bathe him

Rub his tummy and have baby talk with him

But it didn't appear to make him feel better

Sometimes he was ok

Other times he was a hellion

Duncan would often tell me to "fix the baby"

But I couldn't...

I was trying everything

I knew something was wrong with me

When I just stared at Liam while he was crying

"Go ahead and cry, I can't stop you..."

Is one thought that went through my head

Another was "I just wish he was dead."

And at that moment I could clearly see

These weren't normal thoughts I

Should be having about my baby

Something was clearly wrong with me

So, I reached out to my doctor

I told them what was happening

And I stated, "I think I got that postpartum thing"

They asked if I needed counseling

I told them no need

These were just thoughts mixed with frustration

I just needed something to take the edge off

At least until this new kid got adjusted to things

If I was a person that lived in denial

I wouldn't have realized what was wrong with me

Until murder charges were being filed

So glad I was raised to look at myself honestly

If I didn't see myself, I could have just

As easily hurt my own baby

I was all over the place

Trying to work and care for two kids

Dealing with Will and his impeding separation

Wondering how all of this was going to play out

Trying to formulate a new plan

And in dealing with all of this

I neglected to see when life dealt me a new hand

My mom was up to something

I failed to notice

Until I came home from work to see

Me and my kids' stuff on the side of the road

In the very place we were just living that morning

I had no clue what was going on

I went inside and the lights didn't work

This lady just up and left as she'd done to me once before

No words about leaving

Obviously, she didn't care what happened

To me and my babies

I'm still at a loss as to what made her do what she did

Considering the fact that it was me

It shouldn't have been so shocking that she did this silently

But I was hurt that she also did this to my babies

I was in the very thing I wanted to avoid; if I ever had kids

I was now homeless

Homeless with two kids

I'm not doing a very good job at this mothering thing

I'm doing the best that I can

The best I know how

And yet this storm is still hovering over me

I'm sick of the rain

I'm sick of the pain

I'm sick of almost everything

My mother did what she did out of spite

Listening and talking to her second oldest daughter

about how

I was living my life

She took who I was dating so personally

If she didn't like him for whatever reason

That was fine with me

But was her dislike for him worth her putting

Her daughter and her grandkids out on the streets?

That question will forever reside in my head

It's probably something that I will take to my grave

I thought parents were supposed to keep their kids safe

I had no time to feel sorry for myself

I had to figure something out

I had to find shelter for my kids

The only upside was that I wasn't by myself

Will packed his things and left the female he was with

Maybe he did want to be with me

Or maybe he saw that I was struggling

And not just financially

Emotionally as well

I was drowning with no way of saving myself

I found shelter at my workplace

It probably wasn't the best choice

But it beat sleeping in my car

Which I had done with Duncan for a night or two

After my mother secretly moved

I didn't want to trouble anyone

And I didn't have the funds to pay for a room

So, I did the only thing I could do

The whole thing was eerie

Coworkers knew about my situation

And although helpful

Simply by not reporting me to management

At the fact that I was living in a vacant rental unit

It was hard for me to look into their faces

I didn't want people feeling sorry for me

But I had to set that aside

I was doing what I had to do for my babies

Our time was shortened

But what could I have expected

It was my place of employment

I couldn't very well become a tenant

The time spent there was helpful and appreciated

During this time of my homelessness

Will kept a young male cousin by his side

"So they can help out", he said,

Help watch the kids while we worked or stepped out

It was a trying time

So, I figured it was a good idea

One less thing to worry about while we were in the vacant unit

But now, we were no longer there

We found an apartment

We were now in our very own space

Will and I were here attempting to become a family

We'd already overcome so many tragedies

I just wanted things to be simple after the madness

We were trying to settle in

And the more we settled

I wondered when his cousin's tenancy would end

Yes, I was grateful for his help and his time

But it was time for him to go

I wasn't able to relax when I walked through my door

I had no privacy, I couldn't be half clothed in front of this young man!

It would have been different if his cousin was in need

That wasn't the case; he had his own family

A father, mother, and older siblings with their own home

So, this caused a bit of a ripple in the water

Will didn't see it as a problem

He could move around how he saw fit

I was the one who had to walk around in an entire outfit

Will and I were just starting out

We had to figure out how we fit

I had to learn him

And he had to learn me

Once that happened

All would be legit

Everything was coming along

We were settling in our groove

I worked; he worked; the kids went to school

Of course, there were some ups and downs

But overall, things seemed to be coming around

Until things came to an abrupt standstill

While at work Will got injured

There was some sort of accident with a machine he was fixing

Gladly it wasn't life-threatening

But it could've caused permanent issues to his vision

But it was the beginning of the end

Just as loss can bring people together

Loss can also bring people to an end

He was angry because of what happened to him

There was a lot to this situation

There were a lot of things Will was facing

This accident put him out of work

We didn't know how long he was going to be hurt

The situation was serious and he had to get an attorney

Which meant there were more

Responsibilities on me

I knew he was going to need some time

Time to get over the accident

Time to heal mentally and physically

Time for him to adjust to having to depend on his lady

Everything was going to be fine

But time turned out to not be a very good friend of mine

The more time he sat around

The more he was able to do nothing

Nothing but hang out

Drinking and smoking

Now don't get me wrong

I understand different people have

Different ways to release

No need to bring me into the mix

He had his own way of dealing with things

He liked to be around other people

Staying busy… doing things

But some of these things would spill over into our home life

Will was always the "go to guy" in his family

When in trouble call Will… And he would give them whatever

So, another one of his cousins moved in

He was having issues at home

Now I really couldn't be alone

I'm all for helping people

If and when I can

But this was becoming a tad extreme

All this was way too excessive for me

But Will was all for it

After all it was his family

In new relationships I would assume that

They all go through a rough patch

That's all this was

He was used to living a certain type of way

To have people depend on him... it made his day

This was the life he lived before

People moving in and out

His home was a revolving door

And that may have been ok for him at that time

But times had changed

And that would not be a part of my timeline

We were still dealing with his accident

So, I was still the only one working

I was getting sick of it

Sick of housing and taking care of grown-ass people

No room, no food, no money

I was just being realistic about this

And it wasn't just me

My dad couldn't understand how this man was

Ok with having all of these people living around his family

But I held it together

I held my peace…

Because right now, I was the only one sacrificing…

My privacy, my peace, my sanity, and let's

Not forget about my sense of self

When the sacrifice was his

Then maybe he'd see

But until then, my thoughts remained with me

We'd been in our own space for about a year

When our lease came to an end, we moved

Not too much more room in our new place

But there were no extra bodies to house

I felt like I could move; move around freely

In a space that was supposed to be for me

Maybe we could try this again

Create a space with just me and him

Try to get this thing together

Create something solid

So we could withstand all types of weather

And it seemed as if we were headed down that path

Until Will's ex showed up like a big black mass

She darkened any semblance of light

Anytime she came around

She started a fight

She had gone back to work

Because she didn't have to work when she was with him

She needed him to keep the kids

But that wasn't something he was hearing

I told him that it would be ok

If that was how he could help

Then he should...

It didn't matter how he felt

It was an adjustment for him

After all he was used to being the breadwinner

He was used to leaving the kids

Still, after a while, drop off and pick up

On the days she worked was working

Things were moving along

He included them in our family outings

That was until the ex got mad that we were

Having fun with her kids

She constantly created issues every time she came

around

Made me regret encouraging him to keep his kids

She carried on so bad one day

Her own kids told her to leave

They said they wanted to stay

And since then, she manipulated those kids in every way

Although I knew she was encouraging her kids to be

rude

There wasn't much room for me to do anything

Not sure how I would have reacted if I were in her shoes

So, we carried on

Trying to ignore the ignorance

Overlooking the madness

Trying to move forward

I'm beginning to wonder if it's just me

Am I the only one that's going through this?

Why is there always something?

Will had to be the friendliest guy I had ever met

In both of our residences

Multiple people he had befriended

In this new spot there was a lady and her daughter

I guess since they both smoked

He felt inclined to invite them over

So, I was coming home from work and school

To look at two chicks sitting in my living room

As harmless as it may have seemed

I informed him that they viewed me not as his lady

But as a damn sibling

I could tell by how they would look at

I wasn't a threat to their conquest

That caused big ripples in the water

I prepared to square up with this lady and her daughter

I made it clear to him that I better not walk in my home

To these females sitting in here

Without me being present and accounted for

And to bring it on home I asked how would he react if I had

Two dudes in his home while he was gone?

Now, he gets it; now he can see what I mean

Although harmless to him, those females were trying to lay claim

Now another of his family members had to move in

I was a little more accepting of this

She was a single girl with two kids

I sympathized with her

Her parents were much of nothing

One if not both were serving time in the penitentiary

So, I was ok with trying to help this girl in any way

My issue arose with her when I noticed she didn't

Want to deal with her own kids

Her oldest pretty much lived with a friend

And the youngest was on the path of becoming

One of our own kids

If you don't want them or can't take care

Of them, don't have them… It's easy

I was informed, after she'd been with us for some time

That she held onto her youngest

Trying to keep hold of the supposed daddy

And that only happened due to her mom

Selling her to him to get a fix for her habit

The entire situation was sad and numbing to me

But why, in that scenario, would you want to keep that baby?

Either way the child was here

And deserving of a mother who cared

Still, we did our best to meet their needs

But that wasn't enough

I ended up with the entire family

Will offered to help out the girl's mother

Who was being released from jail

But that task fell to me

Will claimed he had other things to do

Obviously, I had more time to lose

Now here I was catering to her needs

While he was off doing whatever

But periodically checking on me

Since the mom was newly released

There was a family reunion

A reunion that cost me

I went to sleep and woke up to a living room full of bodies

This went on for a few days

And it didn't seem to bother him

"It's ok" he would say

"They gone leave"

That time did come

But it wasn't a big jump

They moved less than a block away

Which was convenient for them

They needed a ride to work every damn day

And here again that task came my way

Typical stuff; things were ok sometimes

Other times were a little rough

A lot of outside influences crowded our dealings

He was still not working

Which caused him to sometimes, "be in his feelings"

I didn't think less of him

His circumstance weren't by choice

But by force

So, I figured the little things would help

Drown out some of the noise

His birthday was coming

I planned to create a nice party

Good food... nice environment...

A few of his family

All about him and nothing about me

He enjoyed everything

I was pleased to see a smile on his face

Until it went away a few days later

He felt the need to berate me because

My birthday had now arrived

He was upset that he couldn't do anything for me

He said that I was trying to make him look bad

He went on all day with this

All I could think was

"Is there something I missed?"

It didn't make any difference to me that he

Didn't have the money to do anything for me

If he'd just cleaned up

That in itself would have meant everything

But instead, he decided to 'come out' his mouth

With every mean and hateful thing that came to his mind

And at that moment I knew I wasn't going to be fine

That house with the white picket fence

That perfect picture was only in my mind

I stopped trying to keep up with the arguments

I could shout to the top of my lungs

He still wouldn't hear me

Here I was again trying to create a plan of how to end

And another of how to begin again

I wasn't up for all the senseless arguments

Stupid things about what I said

As opposed to what he thought I meant

There were countless other things

More than what I wanted to deal with

This was only the beginning

He was constantly getting his female cousin's youngest kid

That was an argument…

I repeatedly reminded him that he had his

Own kids who needed him

And it's not that I was trying to be mean

It's just that it was her kid

A kid that she was always trying to get rid of

She created it, she carried it, she had it

And now she didn't want to deal with it

The understanding eludes me – to not to want to deal

With something that came from inside of me

She had no bond with this child

This kid was a bargaining chip; that is all…

A chip that had a nasty fall

Nothing good comes from running behind a man

You can't force or manipulate a person to be with you

This young lady was trying to do just that

She called me crying hysterically

All the while trying to explain something about the child

Because I don't like for bad things to happen to kids

I gathered my own to go and see what happened

To hear what was said

To know that the responsible party was allowed to leave

I'm so glad I didn't have a gun on me

She got into a fight with the guy whilst holding her child

The poor baby fell and hit his head

She was calling for Will to go fight

This guy over what happened

I was floored over what I'd just heard

I erupted like an active volcano

I was spazzing on her due to her lack of concern

Not for herself, but for her kid

She wasn't worried about getting him checked

No concern about what this fall may have done to him

I contacted my kids' dad

And yes, he was also livid

Will came and got Duncan and Liam

And I took this girl and her baby to the hospital myself

If not you... then I will be concerned for this child's health

I mean, visible marks could be noticed

Showing exactly how he landed when he hit that concrete

So how could she not want to take her child to be seen?

This chick showed more concern for what would happen

To the baby daddy than the baby

I had no more words to share

It was obvious that she didn't care

Or maybe she didn't know how

But because of her obvious lack of concern for her kid

The hospital staff had no choice but to do what they did

The case was reported to CPS

That's all anyone needed

This was going to be a mess

Not only for her...

But also, for me...

My kids' dad just couldn't, wouldn't stay away from this baby

Not long after the accident

(Nothing changed with her

She was still trying to get rid of her baby)

She called to ask where we were

We were headed out of town on a family emergency

And she wanted a ride

Again, the baby had fallen and hit his head

She said she would wait until we got back

He told her that it wouldn't be anytime soon

And that she needed to find a ride

Our thoughts were preoccupied by what we were now facing

Tee, which was my best friend and his sister, was chasing after her

Ex-husband trying to get her kids back

We couldn't deal with both

So, we hoped she would do right by the baby

Our trip was an entire mess

But even this mess was better than all the rest

When we got back, we checked on the baby

He was in the hospital

He was hooked up to a machine

We had no clue what was going on

At this point we'd had very little sleep

But we made our way to the hospital

Will needed to see the baby

When we got there, we had no clue

What we were walking into

There were investigators on the floor

Speaking to the parent and grandparent in separate rooms

Trying to gather information to try and figure out

Why this kid was in the state he was in

We were still getting up to speed

We were being cooperative

Until the investigators changed their tone

The family of this kid was trying to intentionally convey

One of a stable loving environment

One the child lived in

That was until the doctors said

That the child would soon be dead

And that someone had to explain

Why this child had swelling on the brain

Upon that revelation

They began to backtrack on the stories they were relaying

Now, all of a sudden, the kid was mainly with Will

They made it sound like he wouldn't let the kid leave

Even in the midst of this mess

Will was refusing to listen to me

I was trying to tell him that this questioning

Was no longer friendly

The investigator had him in the room for hours

I became impatient... suspicious, even

Why were they not speaking with anyone else?

Why had they been in that room for so long?

What in the hell was he thinking, after being in there for so long?

Since he wasn't using logic... I guess it was up to me

So, I started to question what was happening

Yes, I was raising my voice

Yes, I was banging on doors

I had my own kids to worry about

I didn't have time for this nonsense anymore

I didn't know what this all was leading up to

I just knew that we needed to leave

Soon...

The scene was looking eerie

It was quiet on the set

Never in my wildest dreams

Would I have ever been prepared

For what would happen next

I woke up to my normal routine

I got the kids and myself ready for school

I think I was, in some ways, reluctant to go about my usual day

The night before my mind had taken me to another place

I was fighting off these people

They were trying to take my kids

Those thoughts, that nightmare, made me uneasy

But I thought to myself, "that's never going to happen"

I had done nothing wrong and there was no need for me to worry

So, I went on about my day

On the way back from my school

I usually go straight to work

But today I went by the house

Something wasn't right

I checked my mailbox and found a set of keys

I looked up to see my door was slightly ajar

Before I even took a step forward

I called their dad to see if he had left the keys and

maybe forgot

To shut the door

He stated that he gave them to the investigator

They went to look for something

Look for what? was the question that came to me

It didn't seem to alarm him

But me... All kinds of bells were ringing

I walked inside only to see

My kid's room looking like it's been plundered through

But for what reason?

Something came to me and said, "Your dream has come true"

If these people done took my kids

I would have nothing else to lose

So, I called their dad again

I asked if he had picked the kids up from daycare yet

He said he asked my dad to go and get them instead

Now frantic, I pulled into their school

When I walked through the door all

I could remember was the look on the owner's face

And her saying "There was nothing I could do…"

As I watched the tears form in her eyes… I died

It began to rain

Maybe the heavens were crying with me

Because they could feel my pain

Where were my babies?

Who had them?

Someone was going to give me a name

Some lady was trying to talk to me

I didn't know who she was at that time

But I couldn't understand a word she was saying

I left and went to the police station

"Someone has taken my kids!"

This was all I could say

I needed my babies back

And I needed them back today

I turned around just as my dad was walking in

"Somebody took my kids"

The same words uttered to the police I said to him

"Somebody needs to give me my babies back!"

I repeated this over and over again

Then my father looked at me and said

"At least you can get yours back. That girl can't get back her kid"

I had no clue what he was talking about

What in the hell done happened?

And what does it have to do with my kids?

Will showed up to the station

He had gotten news that the baby had died

I calmed down a little

Only because I had to find out what was going on with my kids

Someone explained that they were taken into protective custody

Charges were being filed for the death of the baby

And since those characters said that most of the

Time was spent with Will

They said it wasn't a safe environment

My entire life had been taken from me

My kids were the reason for my existence

I couldn't breathe without them being next to me

And how did Will not know all of this was happening?

He's the reason why they took my kids

I couldn't even get mad

It was hard for me to stop crying

I had to wait on a hearing concerning my kids

Meanwhile, Will was being charged for killing the baby

I'm all alone out here

I'm alone facing my greatest fear

Someone may as well come and take my life

I don't have the strength to breathe

Let alone the strength to fight

I am absolutely nothing without my kids

If I can't protect them from things like this

Then what good am I to them?

I don't deserve to have kids

I've fallen into this black hole

And this fall seems endless

I've sunken to a place where I have no business

Chapter Eighteen

The Sunken Place, Part I

I'm trying to keep it together

I've made it through all types of bad weather

I can get through this

I'm willing to do anything to get my kids back

I'm in a place where I don't want to be

A place where I have no say

A place where I'm not in control

I have to sit back and watch it all unfold

Will was in the same place as me

He could do nothing but wait for the law

To do what they were going to do

I couldn't be there for him

Not the way he may have needed me to

My life had been taken and I didn't know what to do

There was nothing much he could say to bring me back

to reality

I was a dead woman walking

I was barely holding on to my sanity

I managed to keep myself together

Until I was due in court to talk about my kids

I had no clue what I was walking into

I was nervous and I was mad

I prayed that I would be able to wear this mask

The face of a calm individual

One that displayed a concerned, caring face

Not the crazed and insane face

I was trying to replace

I still hadn't seen or spoken to my kids

These people didn't have a clue about all the stuff I was holding in

But I was ready to put on the performance of my life

I going in here to get back the very air that I breathe

My babies will get to come home with me when I leave

I was not expecting what was waiting inside the courthouse for me

It was Duncan's dad, Tim, and his attorney

That mask I had on quickly slipped away

Why was this dude even here?

Now was not the time for him to be trying to play

Any issues between him and me should have had nothing

To do with these proceedings

But for whatever reason that foolishness was allowed

I was getting rules about what I could do and could not do

Where they could go and who they could see

As I was screaming "These are my kids! They belong to me, not you!"

I agreed to things that, normally, I would not have

Like sending Duncan off an extra day with Tim

Even though it had been months since Tim's seen him

And in the midst of all my tears... my begging and pleading

I whimpered "I will do anything… anything to get my kids"

I don't recall ever feeling so helpless in my life

These people had no proof to remove my kids

From my sight

They could traumatize my kids by snatching

Them from their life like it's ok

Not even caring how this may affect them in any way

I knew they couldn't care less about how it was

 affecting me

I cared about their lack of concern for the ones they

took from me

Although it felt like they locked me in a cage

I was getting my kids back

That's all I wanted at the end of the day

They were all I would ever need in this cage I was

 locked in

I had to find another place to live

Charges were filed, officially, against Will

He was locked away, not knowing what was going on

with the kids

I felt bad for him being in there for something he

hadn't done

But my focus had to be on jumping through these hoops

Being overly paranoid about my everyday life

Second-guessing my abilities as a parent

Because now I had social workers watching what I did

and how

Checklist in hand as if hoping I missed something

I lived in a constant state of rage

I saw nothing but red at the turn of every page

It seemed like everyone was out to make a name for

themselves

These were newsworthy events that were taking place

People weren't doing their jobs

They were all just trying to make a case

And Tim was trying to invade my space

He had court ordered visitations that he did not use

He was showing his face with the hopes of Will being

gone

He and I could resume a relationship

He wasn't worried about Duncan's safety

I was living on the edge of insanity

With all these people swarming around me

It was hard to not end up in the same place as Will

I had to stay focused and I did

I found a new place for us to live

And my kids were coming home

I meant what I said about doing anything

So regardless of if I liked it or not I did it all for them

So, when any of those people came around

I was able to muscle up a brief grin

But it couldn't hide the agonizing pain I was in

I could breathe again!

I don't know how many days had gone by

I just knew that today my kids would be in my eyesight

again

Although this situation was far from over

I was going to take this brief moment as a win

They brought my babies out to me...

I could see their relief

We all wept as I fell to my knees

Their embrace never felt so good

Their tears on my face...

Their breath on my neck...

I felt what I felt when they both took their very first

life breaths

I could finally breathe, because they were breathing

with me

I didn't want to let them go

But I was brought back to reality by this CPS worker

hounding me

I had to go over rules and regulations about

What I could and could not do with my kids

Like making sure they had a balanced diet

Decent clothes to wear

No bumps or bruises to be found

So, you gone take my kids if one falls on the ground

I went over schedules for visits for them to check on my kids

It felt like I was signing over my rights to them

The entire process was belittling

As if I didn't know how to be a mother to my own damn kids

But again, I said I would do anything

And anything is what I did by signing

As I felt my babies clinging to me

Some parents don't feel the need to explain things to their kids

Most adults even feel that way about adolescents

That wasn't the case with my kids and I

I raised them to ask questions

To understand the reason why

So I wasn't shocked about all the questions they had for me

I was open and honest with them

Even though they were only 1 and 3

Even though it was killing me

They didn't understand why they were with some lady

They didn't know

Why was I mad at them…?

Why did I let them go…?

This was what my kids were thinking

I had to explain it all

They had to know that it wasn't me

This was all because of what happened with the other baby

We talked as they laid by my sides

They wouldn't go too far from me

My oldest would check to make sure I didn't leave

And that was just for a bathroom break

With a heavy heart

I tried to comfort them as much as I could

I tried to reassure them that everything would be ok

But I honestly had no clue what was heading our way

Too many hands in this pot that was now our life

Phone calls... visits... court dates... follow-ups... interviews

A bunch of fucked-up ingredients in this hell of a stew

As disgusting as it was

There was absolutely nothing I could do

You have people in your life

That were placed there for a reason

They stand by you regardless of the season

One would expect family would qualify as those people

But that's not always true

Hell, it may not even be people

It may be just one person

And that one could be everyone

Keke was that one, and I lost her before this downpour

I lost my best friend

Due to a tragic accident five months prior

I heard about it on the news

Car goes around traffic to cross the tracks

And collides with a train

No crossing gates at this juncture

Which is why it was televised

I caught the very end of it

I didn't know that it was my friend they were
 speaking about

I just knew that it didn't sit well with me

I tried other stations

Trying to catch the story from the beginning

But I couldn't...

Then the telephone rang

Now I was weak in the knees

It was my oldest sister calling to ask me details

about Keke

Trying to figure out if the broadcast was about her

I was going to make sure

And I did...

I went to Keke's dad's house

All he did was open the door

The redness in his eyes had me fall to the floor

The news was true

My best friend was gone

So, this storm without her felt so much worse

She wasn't here with me to yell and curse

I knew she would have stood right by my side

That's what she always did

Still mourning the loss of her while losing my kids

I was a wreck on both ends

I felt like no one could ever fill that void for me

And it was a big void

We'd been friends since elementary

Then the unexpected happened

It seemed to come out of nowhere

It was one of those unforeseen things that come out of the air

My Heavenly Father already knew what was going to happen

He already had a person in place

Yes, I already knew this person

Of course, His plan wasn't clear to me

Janell was a friend... Yes

But my current situation wasn't something that

I would have placed at her feet

But My Heavenly Father did...

He knew she would step up for me

And she did... in her own way

Little by little she showed me that she would be there for me

She didn't force her help on me

She extended her hand politely

I knew how she felt about Will

Janell kept her distance because of the past

Yet, she set all that aside

Even if helping me meant she was also helping him too

I asked her was she sure

Her reply was "That's what friends do"

Nothing else was said

And it didn't need to be

Those four words said

Everything

I got my kids back

I could function a little better

Taking care of them and making sure

They were ok was the only thing that got me through

my days

My thoughts were more aligned

Before, without my kids, my existence was a jumbled

mess

Now it was time to get their dad

I wrote him with an update about the kids

Even though he was in a place where he could do

nothing

I could still see the worry in his face

I needed for him to worry about himself while in jail

I also sent encouraging words

Reassurances that he was going to get out of his

Current state of confinement

And they weren't just words of comfort

I was able to go where he couldn't

Make calls that he couldn't make

I asked questions until I got an answer

The response of 'no,' 'I don't know', 'hold on,' or 'wait'

Was a response that I would not take

A lawyer informed me not to do too much

Or they may decide to charge me

But in my mind, I figured if they hadn't done it yet

Then I wasn't going to let that stop me

My kids were taken and their dad was locked up

While the dead baby's mom was out clubbing

So, I'm about to do the most

These people will get tired of seeing me

This attorney that we dealt with reached out to another

And asked if he would take this case

He vouched for his former client

Made this request as a personal favor

Even though we had our moments

Even though I was ready and planning to end the relationship

This situation proved that Will held a deeper spot than I'd perceived

And to hear and see how this attorney spoke up for him

It reminded me that there was some good inside of him

Regardless of what may have happened between Will and I

Jail wasn't a place for him to be

And as my dad kept reminding me...

"You never turn your back on a person in need"

This person needed me

So how could I possibly leave?

I know there's a saying that

"Everything happens for a reason"

I couldn't see the reason behind this

For this...

Not feeling any divine intervention in this moment

Not sure what good could possibly come from this

I was in constant meetings with people

About this case; about my kids...

For reasons that were still unclear

I didn't understand why the two were intertwined

Any move made against Will

Somehow involved my kids

If taking my kids was to protect them from him

Then why did they keep us under lock and key?

After all, he was locked up

So, what was their real reasoning?

I am far from stupid and nowhere near dumb

So, the reason became clear to me

My kids were being used as leverage in the case against Will

I'm not one that takes kindly to being used

So, to realize that these people were trying to use my kids

Once again, I was livid

This system had no concern for my children

The people of this system are puppets

Employing those with no sense of morals or simple compassion

They were making moves against me

Trying to catch me or even cause me to slip

And no questions were being asked

They still got to cash a check

It didn't matter how many lives they wrecked

So, at this point, I no longer cared

I would no longer suppress my anger

I would no longer force a grimace onto my face

If they wanted to continue to deal with me

Then they would deal with it all

The good... the bad... the disgusting

My thoughts had grown dark

I was ready to lie, steal, and even kill

There was no room in my life, right now, for childish games

I would make them work for everything

They'd been doing all the pushing

So now I would push back

They were not making anything easy for me

And now I would do the same

I was not jumping through any more of their hoops

I have my kids back now

What exactly can they do?

The attorney and I were in constant contact

He was sympathetic of my circumstances

He was appalled by the tactics being used against his client

His assistant felt the same regarding the constant

Threats from CPS concerning my kids

They, too, couldn't understand

What my kids had to do with anything

Through it all they did their job

I got a call saying that Will would be released in a few days

And other calls followed

More rules, guidelines, visits, and meetings

I wasn't allowed to let my kids see Will

They couldn't even talk to him

I didn't want them to take my kids again

So, I had no choice but to comply

The days couldn't go by quick enough

I knew he was ready to get out of that place

It would also be bittersweet

He was free, but not free to look in his kids' faces

Another stipulation upon his release

By no means was Will to live with me

I could only tell him how they were doing or

What they were doing

The entire situation was more bitter than sweet

Hopefully we wouldn't have to deal with this much longer

After all, if they had a solid case

He wouldn't be able to go free...

The day had come and I couldn't wait

It seemed like forever since I'd last seen his face

I was at work, barely able to concentrate

I kept watching the clock

I would be able to see him on my lunch break

While full of joy... I was also saddened

I hated that he had to go through this

I hated that all of this had happened

Hopefully things would get better

This mess would all go away

Hopefully this family would become whole

We would be better because of this someday

My thoughts came back to reality

I glanced at the clock: my lunch break would begin shortly

When the time came, I was gone with the wind

I wanted to make sure I saw his face

I had to make sure he could find our new place

I was so ready to feel his embrace

I was cutting things close

My lunch was about over

But he called and said he was near

Therefore, I waited...

I didn't care anymore about going over my time

I heard a car door close

Then the door to my building opened

We met on the staircase

And in that moment, everything felt normal

All of my anxiety, anger, and worries went away

Even though I knew that feeling was temporary

I took it in and enjoyed it anyway

Even if it was momentary

Chapter Nineteen

The Sunken Place, Part II

Things were still hot and heavy

Their dad was out of jail, but he was still alone

For some reason he didn't want to be around his

own people

Between work and my kids

I didn't have much free time

One would think that he would feel at home

In his own mother's place

But that wasn't the case

Since she wasn't living there

The place was a mess

I assumed that someone would have cleaned it

Up since they knew that he had to come there

And because it wasn't... he was pissed

He wasn't comfortable there

But he didn't have many options

So, when I could, I would go and clean

I only spent one night in jail and could sympathized with

how he felt

I takes a minute to get back to one's self

Considering he was behinds bars for a few weeks

I know he was expecting someone to do something for his pending release

And since his mother didn't think enough to wipe off a little dust

Sent him spiraling down a deep hole

It hurt him when I would have to leave

It hurt when he saw me without the kids

But there was nothing I could do about that

I was dealing with the absence and presence on both ends

Duncan began to ask was Dad – meaning Will – mad at him

He thought that he had done something wrong

And that was why he didn't want to see or talk to them

I tried my best to reassure him that he had done nothing wrong

But I was hurt by his words

I was helpless as well as hopeless

I wanted it all just to go away

I wasn't dealing with my own pain

All of my emotions were bottled up and locked away

I can't deal with them

I have too many other things to face

I was trying to keep it together

I kept telling myself that

I'd been through bad weather

I kept it together then

So, I could keep it together now

I was trying to encourage myself

While my mind was full of doubt

I'd been playing by the system's rules

I had done all that I could do

That didn't seem to suffice

I guess they were allowed to break the rules

Another court date was here

I was not worried; I'd done my part

But this unprofessional CPS worker

Decided to do something she had no business doing

Just so happened that her kids attended the same

daycare as my own

While off the clock

While having no authority

While not informing a worker or myself

This lady questioned Duncan

And from that malicious act

I was thrown into a downward spiral again

She went into court and told what she thought was
 the truth

She didn't confirm any of this information she received from a child

She told the court that I had violated the order

And had allowed my son to see his dad

The court ordered for them to take my kids

No one wanted to listen to facts

No one was interested in the truth

If my son stated that he'd seen his dad

Then that statement was true

He had visitations with his biological dad, Tim

But that point was not acknowledged

She didn't attempt to clarify anything

She didn't admit that she might be mistaken

Even when I explained that he called the person

About whom they were speaking by name –

Will – it didn't make a bit of difference

After all they were, in fact, playing games

As I was trying to explain

As no one was trying to hear my words

As if they were in vain

It took everything for me not to hit that lady

I was loud and crying and pleading to be heard

But I got nothing, because court was adjourned

Because of her so-called authority

They took her words for truth

So now my kids had to be placed with my mom

My visits supervised

Someone had to watch me with my own damn kids

I was now out for revenge

One would think that I would have breathed a sigh of relief

But knowing that my kids were going to be with my mom made

The air difficult to breathe

It may be hard to comprehend

I am aware that it may not even be normal

But I was worried about my kids being with my mother

She presents herself well to the public eye

She prides herself on the appearance of her world

The term "good on paper" is what would sum things up best

She's my mom and I love her

But I do not trust her

Especially with my kids

I know how she is

I know what she is capable of doing... Even to a child

So, my heart wasn't at rest because they were going with her

I called my dad and asked that he make

His presence known while they were there

Show up unannounced

Don't allow her to get comfortable

Don't allow her to think she has time for bruises to heal

Because I know she don't care about knocking the hell out of a kid

He said that he would do what I asked

He assured me that he would make sure my kids were ok

Now, don't get me wrong

I had allowed my kids to be around her alone

Just never for an extended amount of time

A few hours here and there

Overnight a few times out of the year

But this was well after my kids could speak clearly

Clearly able to express anything that may have happened

So, my kids weren't used to her ways...

Her moods... her attitude

Oddly enough, she seemed proud of the fact

That my kids were placed with her

Maybe she thought she could do a better job than me

Whatever the case may have been

It didn't take long for her true colors to show

I got a call from the daycare

Ms. C explained to me how she was seeing a change in my oldest

They wanted to know why he was acting the way he was

What had happened to my son's behavior and his mood

I informed her of what had occurred

What the DSS worker did and said

The court's decision made solely because of it

Ms. C, the owner, was upset to learn what had

Happened under her roof

She confirmed that they knew nothing about the

she-devil speaking to my son

She then explained to me the things my mom had been

Telling Duncan how Will was never coming home

How Will was going to be locked up until he was grown

Then asked if it was ok for her to speak with my mother

As, she stated (and it was true)

They have to care for him for the majority of the day

And they shouldn't have to deal with him

Coming to school that way

And an adult shouldn't be making a child feel such a way

She was right and I agreed

But I knew my mom was going to take it personally

She wasn't going to understand the rationale of it all

So now I was on high alert

Preparing myself for her to claim my son had a

bad accident

She has never been above taking her anger out

on a child

I was just praying that he wouldn't become a victim

The same day or the next day

I got a call from my mom

Upset and wondering why the daycare was coming

at her

She hadn't done anything wrong

Why would my son go and say the things that he said?

She was doing the best she could

Why was everybody targeting her?

How could my son do this to her?

And I sat and listened to her make it seem like

Some sort of conspiracy

Once she was done, I calmly asked

"Why are you telling my son those things?"

She was telling him how the man who has been there

for him

Since he was one, was going to jail

How he was never going to see him again

And only God knows what else she said

But when asked why...

She stated that she was just telling him the truth

"Whose truth?" I asked

I then began to explain to her how my son is a child

How she is not to discuss 'grown folks' business with my kids

Her opinions are just that... her opinions

They are not truths

They are not even based in fact

If that's what she thinks then she needs to keep it to herself or her gossip tree

I did not want, nor did I need for her to be speaking

To my kids negatively

No one was attacking her

Grown folks have conversations about stuff

That's all that it was

Daycare had a conversation with her about simple concerns

Regarding her grandchild

And in the midst of our conversation

It slipped out of her mouth...

She'd been frequently having conversations with the
CPS lady

And when those words resonated in my ears

I FLIPPED OUT

What in the hell was going on here?!

Her title of mother eluded me momentarily

I spazzed on her...

"Exactly what do you think you are doing? That lady is
not your friend. She's lied once, so why do you think she
won't do it again?

What is it that you feel the need to talk to her about?

How do you think this is helping me?"

Not sure why I thought she would finally be on my team

These people weren't my ex

These were some rank strangers at best

But for some reason she saw no harm in speaking
to this lady

The social worker and the guardian ad litem were now
her BFFs

I tried to pound it into her head

These people are not your friends

They are using this situation to try and get ahead

She said "ok," but not convincingly

I know she's my mom and all

But it's about time she met eternity

I don't understand why she does the things she does

Her thought process is clueless

She doesn't appear to comprehend anything

You try not to believe bad things people say about

 one another

But everything my dad ever told me about her appears

to be true

She keeps proving his statements to be true

Even though his intent wasn't malicious

I still didn't want to believe it

But the older I got

The more I saw

Self-preservation can be deadly

And her need to achieve, belong, or appear to do so…

I'm unsure if these were truly her motives

I just knew she was putting her lack of self-esteem

above my kids' well-being

Her need to be noticed was going to have her

somewhere floating

The only reason she was still here

Was because Will stayed in my ear

"Calm down, that's your mom you're talking about"

Is what he continuously said

But I didn't care... I wanted her dead!

A mother would not do something like that to

her own child

Yes, she had done a lot of dirty things to me

But this topped it all

This killed something inside of me

And now I had to go back to court and stand next to her

I had to pretend like we were there on one accord

Clearly, she was not on my side

I didn't know what she had said already

I definitely didn't know what she was going to say

So, I prepared myself for the worst

On the upcoming court day

A lot happened during the time Duncan and Liam were gone

It was tough on my kids to see me come and then go

It was traumatic...

I couldn't keep doing that to my boys

So, I just asked my sister to keep me updated when It came to them

And I stopped going around

As painful as it was for me

I believed it would be easier for them

During that time Will and I were making moves

We agreed the prosecutor and CPS were using our kids as a tool

It was abundantly clear that they weren't in any form of danger

While living under the same roof as Will and myself

They were healthy and happy before they were snatched up

And taken away

So, we decided to relocate to a different county

With the monies from his accident, we bought a home

And since this home was in a whole new jurisdiction

We wouldn't have to deal with social workers and

all of their underhanded dealings

So, we created a home that couldn't be judged

No one could say there wasn't enough room

Inside or out...

We were determined to make things perfect

We would not give them anything to complain about

Will had been going to court-ordered counseling

But we found our own counseling service

We definitely didn't want to use anyone that the courts

referred

Every last one of those people was in cahoots

We weren't taking any chances that the counselor may

follow suit

I'm saying a lot of prayers

I'm asking for a lot of help from up above and from here on Earth

Another day in court

I don't know what kind of stories have been made up this time

And worst of all...

I got to stand next to my mom

I had to wonder who she was even looking out for

The usual antics again

While waiting to be called I was standing in the hall

I didn't know exactly where my mom came from

I didn't know if the caseworker, my mom's newfound friend

Pulled her to the side

I just remember my mom walking towards me like she

Wanted to fight

Apparently, the guardian ad litem put in her notes

That my mom allowed the kids to leave with me unsupervised

And then I allowed them to see Will...

This was clearly a lie (like those before regarding me)

But this lie was about her

So now there was a problem

Now she was upset

Now she wanted to confront folks

Now she wanted to know why these people was lying on her

Now these "some dirty ass people"

All this because of what was said about her

Not once did I recall seeing her this upset

After all they'd done and said about me

But it was a teaching moment

I simply stated, "Now do you see? This is why I kept telling you to

stop speaking to these people and being friendly"

I'm sure she didn't hear a word I spoke

Her focus was set on finding and questioning that guardian

For saying what she said

You would think that I should have been relieved

Something happened that should have brought

my mom to her senses

But history reminded me that

She wouldn't even acknowledge it

To her, sadly, it was no longer about me or my kids

This, again, was a personal attack against her

And she needed to get things straight

Nothing about my circumstances were funny

But at that very moment

I was laughing internally

My mom was out for blood

And it wasn't for the unjust treatment of me

and my babies

Court wasn't terrible

But it wasn't great either

One mission was accomplished...

The CPS case was transferred to a different jurisdiction

I didn't know if things would be any better

But I knew they couldn't get any worse

I was getting my kids back

No more supervised visits

No more not being able to see their dad, Will

The counseling service reported their feelings

And that was... He wasn't a danger to my kids

After all, he did have other children that he was

 still allowed to be around

So that change made me feel a little better

I'm sure those people were glad to not have to deal with

me anymore

I was raising all types of hell

I was knocking on every door

I was calling any number I could call

I was filing all types of complaints

I was deliberately making statements in court

Just so it could be on somebody's documents

Regardless if the judge felt I was out of line

Or my statements had nothing to do with

What was going on right then

I was making sure that court reporter had to type what I was saying

I got a label, due to my actions and behavior

I certainly didn't care…

I was every bit of the label, hostile, that was given

When it comes to my kids

I can say they were quite accurate

With their description

Of course paperwork had to be completed

They had to go through proper channels

The whole song and dance

It was time-consuming

But it all meant my kids were coming home

So, I was waiting anxiously

But patiently

It had been close to six months

Since they were taken from me

At least they saw me a little during that time

I couldn't say the same about their daddy

This moment was a long time coming for him

Therefore, I understood his impatience

After all… he'd been doing nothing but waiting

He couldn't wait anymore to see his kids

I felt his impatience

And I understood why he could no longer hold it in

I reassured him that it was actually going to happen

Moving to a different jurisdiction was proving to be a good choice

Way less chatter on this side

It was too many people on the other end

Multiple visits by multiple people

So many voices when no one was listening

But on this side, it was only one

A good bit of confusion was cleared up with this one

Sadly, I had to reassure this CPS worker that she wasn't in any danger

In regards to me...

Apparently, there was quite a write-up about me

So, to every question she asked

I gave her an answer

I also acknowledged that maybe my responses to the situations were a bit over the top

I explained why I was reacting that way

And to my surprise... she understood my 'whys'

It was such a relief to see

The media coverage of this case didn't have any

bearings

This was an older lady who was just doing her job

She explained what she had to do and how long she was

Required to do it

She didn't understand why my case was still open

But as long as I did my part

She would have no issue closing it

Those words were music to my ears

It was something I thought I wasn't going to hear

There was just one stipulation

Which Will and I both understood

He couldn't be left in the home alone with the kids

Considering it had been close to a year since he'd seen

his kids

That stipulation was one that we could live with

When the day came for me to pick up my kids

I didn't want or need to take nothing from my

mom's house

Nothing other than my kids

Daycare told me they weren't looking like themselves

Nor were they dressing like they were

And that's what I saw when I walked through her doors

My babies were looking so dingy

They looked lost...

But when they saw me, their eyes lit up like a

Christmas tree

As we embraced, they whispered to me

"Mommy, please don't leave"

Before those same words would have killed me

But that day I was able to say

"Y'all get to leave with me"

It was fulfilling to see them so happy

They were ecstatic to hear that they were able to see

Will too

Almost a year seems like forever to a child

They heard me say that and they both went wild

I know I should have shown some sort of appreciation

to my mom

It was just really hard for me to do

I sent my kids to tell her bye and thank you

I knew I would have to talk to her again

But at that moment my words were limited

On the way to their new home

It felt like a big journey

A road trip like in the movies

Everyone was happy and joyful

Although this was my outward display

Inside I was dying... I was hurt

I felt like a failure for letting them get pulled into

 this mess

But it wasn't about me and how I felt inside

It was about my boys with their bright eyes

As I was in my thoughts

We arrived to our new place

I could see the confusion on their eyes

But that all went away

The moment they caught a glimpse of Will's face

Tears were flowing everywhere

He broke down while holding on, for dear life, to them both

I was crying to see how they missed each other so

I didn't rush the process

I just allowed them to be

Be there for each other... in that moment of time

Allowing them, as well as him, to feel that everything was fine

Chapter Twenty

The Sunken Place, Part III: Refusal

This court case stuff began to taper off

It didn't go away...

It just didn't gain any momentum either

We didn't know if they were moving forward with

the case

Or if they were going to drop it all together

My guess and my hope was that they would drop it

Especially considering the fact the prosecutor wanted to

use my child as a material witness

They were relaying information from when

They were interrogating my child

A child with no caring adult present

If this was all the merits of this case was based on

Then all charges should be dropped

I've seen in movies or on TV shows where a side would

do anything or use anyone to close a case

But this wasn't television

This was real life... My life

And I refuse for my son to be used

Things were moving along

There was much of nothing going on with his court case

The CPS case with me, on the other hand, was still

going on

More months went by

More visits from the caseworker

But things were finally coming to an end

One final court appearance

The caseworker had already informed me that

She was recommending the case be closed

My kids were happy, healthy, and in a loving home

All was true and I was grateful that she saw it

Now to prove that the ex, Tim, had no say

Because for whatever reason he was still included

in all this

I had to bring my mom since she was also still a

part of things

And this session was to show and prove why my

kids no longer

Required this so called "protection" from the state

I'm ready to show these folks that there is a different side to me

I'm not just hostile, as they've called me

I'm an undercover lawyer in training

I am all too ready and happy to walk in this courtroom

I am ready to dismantle any shred of evidence

They are hoping to gather from this sideshow

Let's face it, people…

That's all this was; a phishing expedition

We'd already established none of this

Really had anything to do with my kids

Thus, the reason why I sent them with a friend while at court

Didn't trust the powers that be on that day

They won't grab them from daycare like they did before

We were prepared to show up

And I was ready to show out

Bout to show these folks what being a part of my team is all about

The court date had arrived

I was putting my game face on

Will was a little nervous because of everything we'd

been through

But, to me, this was like a championship game

And he had to get his head in the game

We would show no fear or defeat, and I made this clear

to Will

We showed up to the court in sync

No, I did not abandon him... No, I did not switch teams

It was Will and me against the world, along with

his lawyer

Tim showed up with his attorney

I didn't want him there

But since he decided to show up, I was more than

happy to clear the air

The state and Tim's lawyer tried to make Will appear

Incapable of caring for a child...

Until I reminded Tim's lawyer and the state how Will

stepped up

And provided for a son that he did not create

I questioned Tim about how often he paid child support, about how

much child support he was ordered to pay, and who was caring for

his biological son in his clear and apparent absence, financially and emotionally?

I questioned the state official about this protection that they stated

My kids needed – and who did that entail,

Considering the fact that Tim was the one who sent my son home

With bruises from a visitation weekend?

Yes, that statement got an objection from Tim's attorney

Yes, that statement almost got me held in contempt

But were my questions not valid, or was Tim somehow exempt?

Did this not make someone stop and think?

This man can't be all that bad if he's taking on

Another man's responsibility… and willingly

When it was all said and done Will's attorney was glad

We were on the same team

And Tim's attorney could do nothing but shake my hand

My CPS court case was finally closed

I was just waiting on papers

Having papers in hand would make things feel more permanent

There couldn't be any "Oh, I forgot," or

"You must have been mistaken"

No room for any unpredictable movements to be made

I would have documents in my hand to show exact times and dates

My babies were free

No more storm clouds lingering over their heads

They wouldn't have to deal with grown people's messes

No one would touch them or question them

Over my dead body would they ever have to go through this or anything close to this ever again

No one was to be trusted around my home

I was A-OK with having no one coming into my space

Especially no one on his end

Since it was that end that got us here in the first place

I knew that it was just those few

But Will was blinded when it came to his end

Which was the exact reason why I felt this contempt

So, by any means necessary

If there came a time when I needed to clean house

I would do whatever...

Even if that meant putting him out

There were no updates concerning Tim's case

I was telling him to make calls

He was showing no concern on his face

He was still going to counseling for his drug addiction

And yes, people, marijuana is a drug

And yes, one can form an addiction

And he was that one…

It was said to be the cause for some of his actions

 and decisions

During the time in which the baby died

The drug impaired his judgement

Therefore, it was recommended that he quit

It wasn't what he wanted

Yet, something that he needed to do

It was clearly stated "If you test dirty, we will remove your kids"

I was on him to do what was required of him

He didn't like it; and I didn't care

This was something that we could control

It would be hard for him… true

But I was confident that he could

That he would because he cared

The only thing that was in our faces right now

Was him going to counseling and staying clean

I was being supportive and optimistic

I kept reminding him how much this meant

He was cranky at times

Other times he was downright nasty

But I overlooked it all

It was to be expected

He would say that smoking helped him cope

And to be without it was no joke

But I would give up the very air that I breathe

I would take a bullet to ensure my kids' safety

Maybe that's just the mother in me

Maybe it was wrong of me to assume he felt the same

Just because he was their daddy

Turned out my feelings were not shared by him

He let a cousin with no life, home, or family boost

Him up to start smoking again

I understand that not everyone can deal with peer pressure
But when something so important is at stake
How could you make that mistake?
How could his own people claim to care
Yet give him the very thing that could put him back in jail?
And have my kids taken as well?
I was now at a crossroad
This guy was more concerned about getting high
Than he was about his kids
He was sure that everything would work out
He couldn't stop living
I guess since this situation was no longer front and center
He decided he would live as he was in the beginning
Not sure why he was ok with just letting it be
I wanted... No, I needed to know what was going on
I needed certainty
Life was back to some form of normal

It had been several months since we've heard

Anything about a case

We couldn't live life by just waiting

I hadn't come to terms with the fact that my kids were

taken while I was out of town at school

So, traveling that road was not an option for me

I had to find another way to finish my degree

Duncan and Liam were enjoying their space

They'd also eased up about staying in our face

It took a while for them not to worry about someone

coming to take them away

They were no longer worried about mommy or daddy

leaving

But the entire situation had us all on edge

It was so bad that Will and I thought something was up

When Duncan called him 'Dad'

It was a shock to hear

We gave each other a look

It's sad that we didn't know how to handle that

It came out of nowhere

We thought maybe the people from the courts put him up to it

After all, they did create an entire reason from a lie

"He said he saw his dad this weekend"

But back then my child wasn't referring to Will

Again, he'd always called him by name

So, when he didn't…

It seemed as if someone planted that in his brain

Sad to say, but I had to do it

I questioned why did he call him Dad

I questioned if someone put him up to it

This mess had me messed up

But since my kids were able to express themselves so well he explained why he decided to change it up

"When I couldn't see him, I missed him. And he felt like my dad"

He spoke these very words and his words were accepted

And Will was so appreciative of his words too

He couldn't do anything other than hug him and say "Thank you"

Maybe I should have been happy

As he kept stating "No word is a good word"

Whatever that's supposed to mean

To me, no word was just that... No word

No word on what was going on

Was it over or not? Were they building a case or dropping it?

It was over a year

He didn't push the issue none

Happy to no longer be staring down the barrel of that proverbial gun

But in my eyes

What you can't see always proves to be the most deadly

Until one day the phone rings

It was the attorney calling

It appeared that things were 'gearing up' again

They wanted to retrace steps

Go over occurrences

Get detailed accounts of everything that led up to what happened

Now he was no longer carefree

He was jittery and nervous

He was having a hard time remembering

This guy is not worth anything under pressure

All eyes on me when it came to answering questions

The attorney was stating what the prosecution

Was trying to base their case on

Lo and behold they were trying to use the twisted words of Duncan

Prosecution was trying to say that my son told them he was being hit and treated badly

Even claimed he said, "He outed his cigarette on my face"

With no scar to back up this claim

It just proved how they were still trying to play some sick ass game

I didn't need to prove that none of those accusations were true

But I felt compelled to state

"Had he done such things, he would not be sitting in

front of you"

Due to these remarks

Will got mad because he feels like my kid could have

said those things

Because Duncan wasn't his by blood

And he was really bad at believing things that other

people have said

Even though he knew it wasn't true

It still lingered around in his head

Did it cause an argument?

Certainly it did...

I couldn't believe that he was questioning why my kid

Would say something like that

It was difficult to get him to let those lies go

These people would do anything to avoid going to court

I was frustrated by the fact that I had to even go

through this

Me and my kids had taken the majority of this heat

And this was how he acted?

Even after all this

It turned out to be a false alarm

Court was delayed again

These episodes became repetitive

Things would be as close to normal as they could get

Then something about court would come up out

 of the blue

He lost his cool; he had no clue what to do

Something would be said or done

He took his anger and frustration out on me

Then court was delayed

And all I heard was a bunch of "I'm sorry"

Excuses to explain away his behavior

I got that the situation could make anyone feel crazy

But why take it out on the only one standing next to you?

I didn't understand his reasons

But I would just let it go

After all, he was the one facing jail time, not me

I just knew that this case had gone on for way too long

I was ready for this all to be over so we could

truly move on

People never cease to amaze me

And I'm not saying that in a good way

People can appear to be supportive when things are

Good and pleasant

And when they're not…

You have to search to find anyone's presence

This was the case for him and me

Well, mostly him…

Everyone was always in need of him

When things looked good, there they were

But as soon as anything came up about his case

Their presence was scarce

He would never admit that it was unsettling to him

When I would point it out

All he would say was "I don't need them"

But sometimes it's not about an actual need

Sometimes it's about just having someone there

beside you

Even if they are sitting silently

His only need was me

He was fine with just me

I was the one that he had to see

I was the one he was counting on

He was leaning on me

He expected me to be strong

I guess that's ok

But who was being strong for me?

Yes, I was managing things outwardly

Internally I was crying

He was not alone in this battle

For some reason he didn't see that

He became self-absorbed

He was only concerned about himself... his feelings

I was there for him in his time of need

All I needed was for him to spare a little bit of time

for just me

I was going through the same things

And never quite figured out why

He never acknowledged my feelings

"Never turn your back on a person in need"

My father's words sounded off in my head

I would hear him all the time

Especially when I would set my mind to leaving

If I go and he gets locked up

Will it be because of me?

My leaving would surely land him under a microscope

It wouldn't be a regular break-up

It would – could possibly – be used in court

They would definitely twist things

I didn't feel like putting myself in that position

Prosecutors asking me all types of questions

I'd had enough dealing with those people

I would just overlook his actions… his attitude

Maybe he had the right to his own emotional typhoon

I would just have to deal with this storm too

When a person accepts what they can and cannot handle

It can prove to be refreshing

Pretending is not healthy

There's absolutely nothing wrong with verbalizing

One's shortcomings

It's helpful for someone to know your limits

It's ok for a person to actually know when you may need

For them to step in

Or to know when they are overstepping

Neither can occur effectively

If you are always pretending like you don't need

anything... Or need anyone

When that type of behavior is shown

Then you make people think that you can handle things

on your own

But when that moment of truth comes out one day

And you're left there alone to handle things

Now you want to feel some type of way

Now it's "I see how it is! You don't give a fuck about me!"

Although your demeanor constantly shows me how

You don't need me

When I do show up for you

When I do help calm the waters around you

When this wave of madness leaves

When you think that all is ok

You turn and toot your ass towards me

Your actions are repetitive

If it was the straw that broke the camel's back

How much do you think that I can take?

How am I expected to go through your random verbal attacks?

They say you take things out on the ones closest to you

But they never say how those ones are supposed to react

My silence is my solitude

That is the place I'm used to going to

But with Will, my silence seemed to make things worse

I was tired of all the yelling and cursing

Nothing was ever solved

And he wasn't hearing any of my words

I was tired of the screaming matches

It would always take something out of me

So, one particular day I decided to not say anything

Maybe if I didn't make any opposing statements

He would say what he had to say and then it

would be over

I would let him get it off his chest

Then maybe he would feel better

Duncan was at school; Liam in his room

I don't even recall what happened

It was another argument about who knows what

But on this particular day

He stepped things up

He was knocking things over

And to be honest... that really didn't faze me

If he broke it, he'd replace it

My silence was to try and diffuse things

But it did the opposite

He began making his way towards me

Like he was just going to invade my personal space

I never would have imagined what happened next

This dude hauled off and punched me right in my face

Was I shocked....? YES

But my knee-jerk reaction was to grab whatever was close to me

And that something just so happened to be a bird perch

I was now prepared for an all-out brawl

This dude just hit me!

What in the hell was he thinking?

As I proceeded to use my weapon to swing at him

I caught a side glimpse of my baby walking in

I knew he could hear the arguing

But I refused to let him see us fighting

So, I pushed Will out of my way

I grabbed Liam

And I locked us in the bathroom

Seeing my baby snapped me back to reality

But it didn't seem to have the same effect on his dad

He was still ranting and beating on the door

I was in a state of shock. I held my son

Sitting on the bathroom floor

I don't recall how long we were there

I just couldn't believe what had just happened out there

Yes, we'd exchanged words prior

But never had it crossed my mind that he would ever

hit me

It was time for me to prepare my exit strategy

Chapter Twenty-One

The Sunken Place, Part IV:

Mourning

I didn't see myself traveling down this road

A clear path to destruction

And it seems to have accelerated its speed

And I'm not even in the driver's seat

It was the typical apologies

After he put his hands on me

You know, like the ones you see on TV

The "I'm sorry, I don't know what came over me"

Or the "I'll never do that again" apology

None of these words affected me

There shouldn't have been a reason for the apologies

He never should have put his hands on me

He blamed it on being stressed out

And other garbage

None of his reasons had anything to do with me

All I got from his words was that

Since life was beating up on him

He figured he would take it out on me

Since I was taking a beating from life as well

But I was still standing

I guess he felt threatened

Instead of fighting life back

He decided he wanted to fight me

He wanted to control something

So, he decided he would try to control me

And for whatever reason

Some men feel like abuse is the way to achieve it

If I were to say that things got better

And he never tried that again

I would be lying... Things got worse

Of course, there were good days

And then there were days that were bad

Then there were days I wished we'd never had

He began to display this fragile shell of a man

He was needy...

He was insecure...

He was demanding and controlling...

Possessive, persecutor...

Judge, jury and executioner

He displayed all of this

In which, he himself, had never seen

Or maybe he had and was just unable to admit it to me

His arrogance probably wouldn't let him see

He had all these characteristics and more

And all of those conditions

He found a way to project them onto me

I was now a child who needed raising

I didn't have good judgement

In regards to who I should or should not be around

I was unable to think for myself

I was easily influenced by those around me

This was what he now saw when he looked at me

I don't totally get what changed

And why now he had all these problems with me

All I did know was this was going to be one hell of a ride

Because I did not need –

Nor would I allow –

This dude to try and play my daddy

I am far from perfect

I have my own demons to deal with

I know I can be a handful

But I also understand what it means to be committed

I'm a good person...

And yes, one might say I was a good person

I did what I was supposed to do

I didn't follow the typical path of this world

I wasn't the one to go and look for a male's attention

I had friends I'd been dealing with way before Will

But it now was a problem for me to even deal with them

He wanted me to himself

I had to go where he went

I had to be by his side

It didn't matter if I had something to do

Or if I just didn't want to go

He would have a fit until I walked out the door

Slowly and steadily he was trying to take free will

from me

There was nothing that I could do for just me and my babies

Play dates were not a thing

Janell and I would hang out with our kids

Until after a while he had a problem with it

But it was ok for us to sit around a bunch of grown folks

In their element

I just knew something had got to give

Will wanted me around only the people he knew

People I had nothing in common with

But there was an issue: I had little or no words to speak

I was embarrassing him

He was asking me what was wrong with me

I would speak when I was spoken to

Not sure what else he wanted me to do

This occurred with several of his family members and his

One female friend

They all smoked or drank or both

I didn't fit in...

I'd been me since he'd known me

I couldn't understand why he was so hell-bent

On trying to change me

Will surely wasn't interested in changing anything

about himself

So why should I do a 180

Just to make him feel comfortable with his manhood?

What other reason would he have to be

Continuously coming at me the way that he did?

I was good to him…

Hell, I was good to his disrespectful-ass kids too

Always trying to talk back

Constantly lying that I'd done something wrong to them

But upon his request to let it go… I did

I didn't know what else it was

What else did he want me to do?

I worked, went to school, took care of the house

And kids too

I supported him when he needed me to

Was it too much to ask to get a little of the same?

No matter what or how much I gave

It never seemed to be enough

He would find a way to mess it up

He would complain that I didn't make time for just him and me

But when I tried, he spent half the time trying to

Find some 'good weed'

When he would complain about what I didn't do

For example, making breakfast for him after working third shift

I tried to oblige

And even that wasn't pleasing to him

The more this occurred

The less I liked him

The less I liked myself

It felt like I was at a point of no return

I'm starting to not recognize myself

I'm becoming the very thing I used to despise

A person living with, dealing with, staying with someone

Who's abusive

That childhood saying from my younger days

"sticks and stones may break my bones, but words

will never hurt me"

My dad used to explain how this was a lie

"Words can hurt you," he said

Which is why he wouldn't allow us, as kids, to

Call each other names

But in my current situation

The words brought the most pain

Abuse can appear in many forms

Not just physical

But verbal and emotional abuse

Which can leave just as many bruises

That was my daily struggle

That was the most draining

Defending myself against his words

When someone else did him wrong

Or he had a bad day on the job

Or life was just hard…

He and his words would put us at odds

He would get downright belligerent

When I would take up for myself

Because I didn't believe this portrait

He was painting of me

He would try his best to force these insecurities

upon me

No... I'm not a whore!

No... I'm not gay!

No... I'm not messing with these minors who

ride to work

With me every day!

No... I don't have daddy issues!

I need no man to raise me

No... I'm not a bitch! I don't walk on four legs

And no, I don't go "in heat"!

Then, when the tables turned and I screamed and yelled

Then it was "Baby, I'm sorry, I didn't mean any of those things"

How is it that a person is able to repeatedly say things

That they don't mean?

"The mouth speaks the matters of the heart"

That's what I'd read in my readings

So, I told myself, "lady, he means every

word of what he's saying to you"

There was absolutely nothing I could do to change

his views

And because of that fact I sank a little more

The court case was still lingering

So, whenever we got into it

I wouldn't, couldn't cause him to be locked up

Regardless of the charges he already faced

It would be my fault if he ended up in that place

The good days were few and far between

With every breath he took

He found a problem with me

He took issue that I didn't have a picture of him in my phone

(A phone that was off and hadn't been used in months)

So, to extinguish that argument

I tossed the phone in a sink full of water

He had a problem, another time, with my phone ringing too much

So, while he was driving, I threw it out the window

Now there was no need to fuss

But that gesture backfired on me

The people whose yard it landed in called the numbers in my phone until

They spoke to someone who could get a hold of me

My long-time friend, Ann, emailed me

I called her using his phone

As I spoke with Ann, he stood right in front of me

He was upset because I told her the truth

"You just trying to make me look bad!" is what he said

There was no lie for me to tell

No lie could explain why a stranger ended up with my phone

He had a problem with my reading of books

So, I would only read when I was alone

He had issues with my going to school

I was messing with all the girls and the one guy in my class

He acted as if he didn't want me to work

He always accused me of cheating

He even tried to follow me to work one morning

He left our kids home alone asleep

To see if he would catch me cheating

And he supposedly did all of this because he loved me

He had issues with me not holding conversations with

His people at functions

But when I did become friendly

It meant I was up to something

He would have all of his male family members around me

Then question if they were hitting on me

His paranoia and possessiveness were sickening

I began to truly isolate myself

He had issues with me going around my own family and friends

He would threaten to do vindictive things to them

So, I limited my involvement with them all

I was already at the bottom

I couldn't sit and watch them fall

And even that wasn't enough for him

He now had issues with how much time I spent with my... our kids

Too much time with them and not enough with him

I was at a loss for words

This scenario I would have never imagined

I'd heard of people having multiple personalities

It wasn't something that I'd seen personally

But having dealt with this dude

And his ever-changing moods

I began to wonder if Will suffered from some form

Of mental instability

A "normal" person can't really have that many mood swings

A "normal" person can't make up stories and believe

them to be true

A "normal" person can't hate you one second

And in the next say "I love you"

None of this made sense to me

The sight of him would, sometimes, make me sick

Sometimes I would look in his direction, but

Not directly at him while speaking

Oftentimes I would go to this place of misery

While there I didn't care what was happening

I didn't care what came out of his mouth

I didn't care if he was trying to be nice to me

Nothing regarding him mattered to me

I found myself wishing he would get locked up

Just so I could be free

And just to have that thought cross my mind was sad

I had no right to wish that upon him

Wishing for him to lose his freedom

Just so I could 'be free'

Maybe I was the one with multiple personalities

That time had come again

Phone calls were coming in from the attorney

The same song and dance all over again

Going over timelines

Checking various statements

Interviews with private investigators

Gathering information to track potential witnesses

My distaste for him left me

He was afraid, worried, hurt…

He was vulnerable here

He was scared he was going to lose me

He was emotional and apologetic

And no matter how mad I was at him

I would always reassure him that we were in this together

"I will be here until you make me leave"

Those words of comfort would put him at ease

It helped him better prepare himself for what we

Would soon be facing

Or so we thought, that it would be soon

But here again... the case was continued

A bunch of back and forth

That's what my life had become

The same thing over and over again

An emotional rollercoaster that never ended

Didn't know where the good days began

Or where the bad days ended

I was in a state of mourning

Mourning the death of self

Someone was looking back at me in the mirror

But she was unrecognizable

Nothing about her reminds me of me

The me that I used to be

I was on guard constantly

I was not pretending to be nice around company

I was always angry

Waiting for someone to do or say something that would piss me off

It always seemed to happen

So, I decided to always be ready

I had no reason to be friendly

Many of Will's family constantly came to my house disrespecting me

His kids continued to tell lies on me

Roll their eyes at me while I was talking

They even tried to swing at me

Only because those actions were tolerated by other people

Other members of Will's family had negative words about me

Only because I required him to take care of his family unit: us

I wasn't about to have every member of his family living with us

This was his life before there was an us

I was tired of him being the host, the life of the party

People showing up empty-handed

And he was ok with it

It wasn't coming out of his pocket

So, it seemed to be no bother

I was constantly under attack

And when I would react...

He would always tell me

"You shouldn't act that way. Don't follow up with their ignorance"

But those words only went one way

Never got why he expected so much from me

And nothing from those he called his friends and family

It was always left up to me to ignore the comment

To ignore the actions

To be the bigger person

To not be so nasty

"Why you gotta be that way?"

He would ask me and just me

So I questioned him, "Why you never ask them to stop messing with me?"

His reply would never be direct

He never stated what was actually said

It was always "I don't care about them"

But he actually did

If he didn't then it wouldn't have been so hard to "pull their card"

Which led me to believe

He was more concerned about them and their feelings

I was done with the battle

I didn't care if I won the war

There was no getting through to him

I no longer cared to try anymore

And in the midst of another fight

I found myself on the floor

And in mid-tussle I gave up

I didn't want to go through it anymore

So, when he put his hands around my neck

I saw an opportunity…

"Just let him do it. Imma just let him kill me"

Things went black

But the darkness was short-lived

When I came to, I saw him over me

And I started swinging

Many moments have raced through my head

There have been several times I've wished I was dead

There have been many times I've tried to make those wishes come true

There were many times that he'd pull a gun on me

And I'd ask him to pull the trigger

To do me a favor

To just end things for me

Other times it just pissed me off

Because he was doing it to try and scare me

I have done things

I said I would never do

I have dealt with things

I said I would never deal with

I think I've gone as far as I can go

He's not trying to do better

Actually, he's getting worse

He was staying out all night

He put a lock code on his phone

He was hardly ever home

The sad part is, it really didn't bother me when he didn't come home

My issues came when he started lying to me

If I ask a question, then be man enough to answer honestly

When he looked me in my eyes and lied to me

That's when I made it up in my mind to leave

And although I'd made my mind up many times before

This was the final straw

I was really prepared to walk out the door

I didn't have much of a plan

I just knew things wouldn't be civil with this man

I had tried to leave before

I had a place secured

Even had the keys to the door

But I messed up when I showed my kids

Not really thinking about the consequences

I couldn't fault them for speaking on the subject

Which is why my leaving this time would be abrupt

I didn't have time for the tears

The guilt trip or his fears

We had bought a second home during our ups and downs

Our first home was vacant

And with a few dollars in his pocket

He thought he had it going on

His actions and his lies confirmed he was a cheat

I went through his phone and saw it all

He'd found him someone new

When I questioned him, I just wanted to see if he would tell the truth

So, it shouldn't have bothered him if I left

I'd gone as long as I could

I'd dealt with more than I should've

I tried being supportive of him

I catered to all of his needs

I dealt with different forms of disrespect

But this form of disrespect eludes me

Staying out all night with no communication

I remembered something I once read

"You deserve what you tolerate"

And that got me thinking

It meant I couldn't blame anyone but me

I tolerated him...

I tolerated his mess...

I tolerated all of the foolishness...

So, did I get what I deserved?

I allowed all of this to happen to me

Trying to be a good woman

Trying to have a family

But as my father told me

"It's better to leave than to have your kids grow up in a home where you're not happy"

I could no longer stay until his court case was over

Perhaps this was punishment for me killing my babies

So, with that realization... I accepted it all

I deserved every bit of it

What I'd gone through was all my fault

If this was my penance...

Then hopefully I was done

Right now, I thought, I have to go…

He's setting too many bad examples for my sons

I love him and I probably always will

But I can no longer allow him to treat me this way

It's about time for me to heal

Chapter Twenty-Two

Released

When you go through things in your life, you expect a certain outcome. With the childhood I experienced, I came to expect difficulty and hardship. Yeah, I know I said I had goals, that I had a plan, and I did, but none of those "certain outcomes" came to pass. Since jail was ever-present growing up, I expected to get locked up. In my mind it would be for something minor, like shoplifting. Never in my wildest dreams would I have imagined actually catching the charge that I did. I can only tell you that it was eye-opening. Imprisonment is not for me.

My childhood was just that, sometimes; a child in the hood. My eyes saw things they shouldn't have seen and the majority of the people were no good. When you are always around certain things, it can become the norm. Well, my dad informed my siblings and I daily that this life wasn't normal. That saying, that "kids do what they see, not what you say," doesn't have to be true. Although I grew up around a bunch of chaos, I knew I wouldn't have been able to handle it on my own. At times life was an uncertain hell, but it was ok because my dad was there. His words follow me to this day. If not for him I would have wasted away.

He was my rock, my guiding light, my counselor, my beacon of hope. He was indeed "my superman," even though he was an addict. His addiction didn't minimize his parenting. He was a force to be reckoned with. And in my eyes, that meant everything. He had his faults, as many of us do, but he had a big heart. He was protective of his own. No harm could come our way. He did his best. Which is all anyone could do. He required the best from us, and I was determined to fill those shoes.

I now know my mind was at war with itself. Consciously I wanted better, but subconsciously I expected less. I knew everything I didn't want to be. I knew what type of career I wanted. I knew when I wanted to marry and have kids. In my mind, I'd created the perfect life. But deep down the dark side knew that wasn't going to happen.

I allowed myself to take chances. To do things just because I expected that of myself. It was self-sabotage, but back then I didn't know the meaning. So, my stupidity landed me in a bad spot. In my mind I could get away with it; there's no way I could get caught. It was easy money. I now know that there's no such thing as easy money. I think that time of incarceration, however brief, made me realize that I had to change my way of thinking. There was absolutely no way I could make it on two totally different paths. That time in jail showed me my life if I chose to stay on my current path. So, I tried to drown out the subconscious thoughts. I don't want to say it was too late, but I will say it was one hell of a fight.

It took years for me to change my way of thinking. I still have my moments, but I can change my thoughts more quickly now. I now understand the meaning of self-sabotage. I now know that the circumstances of my upbringing don't define me. It doesn't have to be a road map to my future. It can't hinder me. It can and will only breathe as much as I allow it to. So, it occupies very little of my room. Why I didn't just block it all out, you say? It's simple… I need a constant reminder not to go back that way. It's my personal detour sign. I feel like not knowing or remembering makes it that much easier to press rewind. I work on my thoughts daily. It's a conscious effort. Who, on this earth, knows me better than me? And I know that this is what I need.

Relationships are difficult. I viewed having an intimate meaningful relationship to having a good friendship. I've always told myself, "Whoever the guy may be, he should be a friend before anything." To me, in my world, friends don't argue. They will have disagreements about different issues, but they share a foundation. A friend is there regardless. Your mistakes... your flaws... they don't bring them up. Still, will they hold you accountable for your stupid moves? Indeed. These were qualities I figured should be in a relationship best suited to me.

I didn't want to argue in my relationship. We could disagree and I wouldn't hold it against him, nor him against me. I believed we were supposed to be solid. I truly thought this was an attainable goal. Maybe those thoughts were naive. After all, I've never seen this type of relationship outside of TV. I was basing this on the fact that I had close male friends. We got on each other's nerves, but we were always cool in the end. So, I didn't think my perspective was too far of a reach. I didn't realize how far it was until I actually started dating.

I never found a guy on my own. It was always a friend that initiated my approach. I knew nothing about flirting. I'm not all that 'girly,' so dating was unfamiliar territory. But if you guys remember, I had myself a timeline. I'd reach certain points where the time had come for certain milestones to occur. I now see how detached from reality I was. When it came to the relationships I was in, I now see that, initially, it had nothing to do with the person themselves. I can't sit here and say that it was some deep attraction to any of them. I was so used to only being in my own head. The things that women were supposed to do went right over my head. I didn't care if the guy called. It didn't bother me when they said we would do something and we didn't. It's quite possible that the first two partners (of which Tim was the second) loved me in a way I neglected to see. With the first, Hugh, I figured we were both too young to understand what love truly meant. Which is why I dismissed his feelings. I cared, but now I think that's all those two got from me. It surely wasn't the deep friendship I was seeking. Honestly, I think it was just something to do. Which is why it didn't bother me when I ended things. Yes, I shared a child with Tim, and it bothered me by virtue of my becoming a "baby mama", but I didn't feel like I lost the love of my life. The one that I can say I was in love with turned out to be my most devastating relationship.

To me, love should be genuine and pure. It's not supposed to hurt. It shouldn't be something a person endures. Love should be welcoming and carefree. To love and to be loved should come naturally. I thought this was what was developing in my last relationship, number three: Will. I would cover him, and he would cover me. We would create a solid unit. One that no one or nothing could break.

I thought we were on the same page, but he soon made a liar out of me. He was only concerned about himself. His main interest was what made him happy. He was all for me covering him, but not too much about covering me. My relationship with him seemed to be one-sided. You can't continuously take and give nothing in return. Even if all you can give is gratitude to the person treating you good.

I learned a lot about myself during my time with Will. I learned that although I made mistakes, I am a loyal person. I can be fearless at times. I am dedicated to those around me. I am selfless. Although these are good qualities for a person to have, I sometimes wonder if they played a part in my downfall.

I once heard a radio show on which they were speaking on failed relationships. And the speaker summed my relationship up in one sentence. She stated, "The very thing that attracted you to me, is now the very thing that makes you dislike me." That statement made things so clear. This is why Will was hell-bent on trying to change me. He loved the thought of me, but he didn't like having to put up with me. All these good qualities that I possess, and sometimes question, made him uneasy and incapable of engaging me.

I knew that I had lost the last little piece of myself when I was with Will. My dealings, my choices, my actions, my attitude, and my overall acceptance of the mess proved that I no longer loved the person looking back at me. I've done things I said I would never do. I said I would not be that woman that stayed with a man after he's put his hands on her. I didn't want to be a "baby mama" to any man. I have become all these things and more. I couldn't stand to be in my own skin anymore.

So, what is love? Because of what I've been through... love is nothing. It hurts too much. It leaves eternal scarring. I don't think most people have the same meaning of the term. However saddened I am to admit it, love is a four-letter word to me. I will have to relearn the meaning of that word one day, but that day is not near. This will be one of my growing pains. When the time comes, I will put forth a valiant effort, but for now I will give the thought of love a much-needed rest.

Here I am, my friends. Here I go, starting from scratch again. When I left my last relationship, I can admit that I was angry and hurt. I mean, I'd intertwined my life with this man. But I refuse to let it define how I move on. How I carry on. I am in the process of finding myself. She's been missing for so long. I know that I'm going to need some help. My father always told me, "Life owes you nothing! It's designed to beat you down to your knees, but it's left up to you to get up again and to keep moving." So, I'm up and I'm moving!

It may take me a while to get back on my feet, but I will stand independently. I found me a team to assist me on my quest. I know that I've surrounded myself with those who will push me to be my very best. I'm learning that "I" is not the best term for me. "I" made a lot of mistakes trying to take everything on alone. "I" didn't have control of anything. So therefore, I left "I" alone. It's now My Heavenly Father, and then me. I'm learning to wait on Him. He has something great waiting for me. He is helping me realize who I am truly meant to be.

My aspirations weren't all that bad; I now see. I just didn't have the right partner standing beside me. I'm no longer looking for anyone on this earth. The One who put me here has shown me my worth. I lost sight of that in the midst of my countless tsunamis. Now the vision is clear! I understand my purpose. I know why My Heavenly Father allowed me to remain here, physically as well as mentally.

I went through all that I have, just to get here. To share various tidbits of my life with you. And no, this wasn't all of it! This is just what I could get through. I want it to be known that the circumstances of your life don't have to define you. By all accounts, I should probably be dead or in jail. All that I've been through; all of the multiple levels of hell, I wouldn't change a thing. From the center of all that mess out stepped a stronger young lady.

I'm only human. I still have my faults. But I can handle myself better now. I know who to call on. Yes, I have a ways to go, but I'm actually looking forward to the journey. Peace of mind is priceless! Never again will I allow her to be taken. I will no longer set her to the side to appease anybody. No one can pay me anything for the look on my face when I see the woman looking back at me.

I'm done dulling my shine. I now know and understand that I was placed in Will's life, in that position, for a reason. It's written that things only last for a season, and that season of my life is over. I can co-exist with Will. I can even laugh and talk with him. I can return to my very own space and not have to deal with him. I have forgiven him so that I can be free.

I was told by my pastor, "Never regret doing good for a person. It's up to that individual how they receive your goodness." So, with that in mind, I don't regret any of the good that I have done or tried to do for any person that I have crossed paths with. It takes too much energy to be mad at those who didn't return the favor. Which is why I don't hold on to any of the bad in my life.

I could have easily let my numerous tragic situations mold me into a very different person. I could have used my circumstance and upbringing as excuses for me to become a spiteful, vindictive woman. But why should I? How long can I blame my past for my present or my future? My answer to that question is... I can't!

I once heard an expression: "excuses don't excuse and explanations don't explain." I may, to some, have justifiable reasons to excuse any bad behaviors I could display, because of my life and all I've gone through. But it's just that... my life. So, I decided to embrace the bad, the terrible, the pain, the anguish, the failures, the hurt, the tears, the fears, and the hopelessness. All of these things and so much more, I use to fuel the fire of my journey to wellness and joy. I have chosen to no longer just survive this life. I am now looking forward to actually learning how to live this life.

I love myself again. I like what I see. Everything that could have, that should have broken me has made me. I have endured a forty-year war, people, and I am thankful for it all. I am thankful instead of regretful, and I truly believe that is why I wasn't allowed to fall. Yes, it was a slow and dreadful process, with a lot of ups and downs, but I got back what I left and so much more. More peace, more of myself, more positive "life lessons" for Duncan and Liam, more time to enjoy the life I'm now living in a safe space.

I am so good, y'all!

www.ingramcontent.com/pod-product-compliance
Lightning Source LLC
Chambersburg PA
CBHW021138160426
43194CB00007B/622